Andrew Jackson

Andrew Jackson

MARGARET L. COIT

MARSHALL CAVENDISH
CORPORATION

GREY CASTLE PRESS

Published by Grey Castle Press, Lakeville, Connecticut.

Marshall Cavendish Edition, North Bellmore, New York.

No part of this publication may be reproduced in whole or in part, or stored in a retrieval system, or transmitted in any form or by any means electronic, mechanical, photocopying, recording, or otherwise, without the written permission of Grey Castle Press.

Published in large print by arrangement with Houghton Mifflin Co.

Copyright © 1965 by Margaret L. Coit.

Format, this edition, copyright © 1991 by Grey Castle Press.

Printed in the USA.

Library of Congress Cataloging-in-Publication Data

Coit, Margaret L.
    Andrew Jackson / by Margaret L. Coit.
      p.   cm. — (American cavalcade)
    Reprint. Originally published : Boston : Houghton Mifflin, 1965.
    Includes bibliographical references and index.
    Summary: A biography of the hero of the War of 1812 who became the seventh president of the United States.
    ISBN 1-55905-082-9 (Grey Castle : lg. print)
    1. Jackson, Andrew, 1767–1845—Juvenile literature. 2. Presidents—United States—Biography—Juvenile literature. 3. Large type books. [1. Jackson, Andrew, 1767–1845. 2. Presidents. 3. Large type books.] I. Title. II. Series.
[E382.C67 1991]
973.5'6'092—dc20
[B]
[92]   90-48986
                                                                                                CIP
                                                                                                                            AC

ISBN 1-55905-082-9
     1-55905-100-0 (set)

Photo Credits:

Cover: Library of Congress
Library of Congress—pgs. 9, 19, 96, 162, 168
Brown Brothers—pgs. 30, 126
The Bettmann Archive—pgs. 72, 136
North Wind Picture Archives—pg. 64

Contents

★

Chapter 1	Fifteen Years to Grow Up	7
Chapter 2	The Gentleman from Tennessee	16
Chapter 3	Code of Honor	26
Chapter 4	War: Public and Private	37
Chapter 5	Redcoats and Redskins	46
Chapter 6	Victory at New Orleans	56
Chapter 7	The Democratic Candidate	71
Chapter 8	Jacksonian Democracy	93
Chapter 9	The Union Preserved	110
Chapter 10	The Battle of the Bank	128
Chapter 11	The Last of Triumph	144
Chapter 12	Texas	152
Chapter 13	Death of a Hero	164

| For Further Reading | 171 |
| Index | 172 |

1

Fifteen Years to Grow Up

BACK IN 1767, up in the rolling red hills of the old Waxhaw country, nobody knew or cared whether the cabin of George McKemey stood to the north or south of the shadowy line where the Carolinas met. It was nearly a hundred years later, when only a pile of hearthstones under a grapevine remained to mark the site, that the question was even asked and it was decided that the cabin lay north of the line. For it was here on the night of March 15th that Andrew Jackson, who was to become the seventh President of the United States, was born.

He was born a poor relation. Only a few weeks before, the body of his father was jerked down in a farm wagon to the old Waxhaw churchyard, and there among the "rude stones" laid in an unmarked grave. The family had woven linen cloth back in Carrickfergus, Ireland, and the elder Jackson had worn himself out clearing and working the unbroken land up on Twelve Mile Creek, land that he was too poor to own. After the birth of her third son, Andrew, Mrs. Jackson earned their board by becoming a housekeeper in the home of her brother-in-law, William Crawford, over the line in South Carolina. Here in a country of old, overgrown fields and giant pines whose roots scarred the red roads, young Andrew grew up.

Nearly a hundred years later old-timers still recalled tales of the barefoot, redheaded boy who had been the holy terror of the neighborhood, fighting, racing, overturning outhouses and bullying the bigger boys. "Andy," they still called him. "When Andy was President," they would say, or, "When Andy was at New Orleans." They remembered that he suffered from "slobbering" and "the big itch," and this made him touchy and hard to get along with. A strong boy could throw him down easily, but "he never would stay throwed." Once some boys teased him by giving him a big gun to fire. The recoil knocked him flat. He sprang up, his brilliant blue eyes blazing. "If one of you laughs," he shouted, "I'll kill him!" No one did. No one was ever to laugh at Andrew Jackson.

He went to school in a log shanty in an "old field,' and learned to read, to figure, and to write.

Born on March 15, 1767, a few days after his father's death, Jackson lived with his family in a log cabin in the Waxhaws—a rugged, hilly region on the border between North Carolina and South Carolina.

He never learned to spell. Latin he would quote occasionally, though he knew only a few words and phrases. He could never write English correctly, although in later life he often wrote it passionately and with eloquence.

But in those days, it was a great thing to know how to read. The first big moment of Andy's life came when he was nine and was requested to read aloud. The year was 1776, and Andrew Jackson read his neighbors the words of the Declaration of Independence. When the Revolution finally burst in a red hell over the area, Andrew Jackson knew very well what he was fighting for.

At thirteen, he was tall as a man, but overgrown, spindling and frail. He was always to look upon himself as a soldier of the Revolution, though it is doubtful that he was ever formally sworn onto the Army rolls. His oldest brother Hugh enlisted, and died of heat and exhaustion after a hard-fought battle. At first, when the British Lieutenant Colonel Tarleton and his Raiders swarmed over the Waxhaw country, the Jacksons moved northward.

Andrew was disappointed. Someone heard him burst out as he cut weeds: "Oh, if I were a man, how I would sweep down the British with my grass blade," and the neighbors said that here was a boy who would "fight his way in the world." He had already looked upon the harvest of war, the "dreadfully mangled" wounded men whom his mother nursed in the old Waxhaw churchyard. "Some had as many as thirteen wounds and none less than three."

The British moved on, and the Jacksons returned to their ravaged neighborhood. But the fighting continued and it was ferocious now—brother against brother, neighbor against neighbor. The settlers from the Scottish Highlands were Tories and fought for the King; the poor

Irish were Whigs and revolutionists. Andy and his other older brother Robert joined a band of Whig guerrillas. Years afterward, a neighborhood girl remembered a lanky, dust-covered forlorn-looking boy, on a wild pony, whom she asked for news of the war. "Oh, we are popping them still," was Andy's cheerful answer.

Caught in a raid, the boys took refuge in a relative's house, where a bitter Tory informed on them. The British burst in, wrecked the furniture and china, and herded Andrew and Robert away. Then came the final humiliation: they were ordered to black an officer's boots. Andrew refused; he was a prisoner-of-war, he said.

The officer lunged with his sword as Andrew's hand flew up. The boy's hand and his head were cut to the bone. He was to bear those scars and his hatred of the British all his life. A moment later Robert was struck to the floor, so savagely that he never wholly regained his senses. Then the two dazed and bleeding boys were thrown on horseback for a forty-mile ride to the prison stockade at Camden, South Carolina.

There was smallpox in the stockade, the most dreaded and loathsome disease of the time. No one cared. No one on either side cared anything about prisoners except for taking them. There was no food except moldy bread, no medicine; even the prisoners' good clothes were stolen. Young Andrew heard the men moaning and cursing through the night; in the daytime he had to watch them die.

Help was on the way. Young General Nathaniel Greene, who had fought the British General Cornwallis to a standstill at Guilford Court House, North Carolina, arrived with his army in April, and took a stand on Hobkirk Hill. Secretly, in the night, Andrew hacked a hole in the stockade wall. The next morning, horrified, he watched Greene's unprepared men eating breakfast and cleaning their guns, only to be blotted suddenly from his sight by the sudden smoke of musket fire. The British were upon them. Watching the tide of battle ebb and flow, Andrew learned a major lesson of war: to stay alert. All hope vanished among the prisoners, as the trapped Americans disintegrated into a wild mass of riderless horses and retreating men. After seeing this disaster, Andrew looked forward to nothing but death. Then, suddenly, he found himself rescued. His mother had not forgotten him. The undaunted, blue-eyed little woman had come forty miles to Camden, gained an interview with the British commander and persuaded him to exchange her sons and five Waxhaw neighbors for thirteen Redcoats that the Americans had captured.

For Robert the help had come too late. He was so ill with smallpox that he had to be held on his horse. Andrew, although gripped by the icy chills and burning fever of the disease, walked the forty miles home, the last hours in a cold downpour of rain. Two days after they arrived, Robert was dead and Andrew delirious. It was months before he was well again.

As if she had not given enough to her country and the Revolution, Mrs. Jackson had to do even more. After Andrew had recovered, she went down to Charleston to nurse the American men on the British prison ships. All his life, Andrew treasured—and probably glorified—her last words to him. "You will have to make your own way," she told him. "None will respect you more than you respect yourself. . . . Avoid quarrels . . . but sustain your manhood always . . ." It was almost as if she foresaw her end. For she never returned. She caught fever in Charleston, died, and was buried in an unmarked grave. She would have been forgotten forever if the world had not heard of her son.

As for Andrew, at fifteen his childhood was over. He had known misery and poverty, death and war. Overnight he had become a man to whom war meant a single thing: the hard business of killing. And with the long strain of the conflict over, he availed himself of the privileges of manhood. He was earning his own living, first as a saddler's apprentice, and for a brief period, even teaching school. Someone left him a small inheritance, and at the same time he became friendly with a group of young bucks from Charleston. Suddenly he gained an unfortunate taste for their amusements: horseracing, cockfighting, drinking bourbon whiskey, and betting at cards. With his Scotch-Irish relatives grimly predicting that he would come to a bad end, Andrew followed his expensive new friends to Charleston. There having spent or lost all but his horse and saddle, he gambled them on a bet, won, and abandoned Charleston forever. He had learned wisdom early.

But he did not return home. Instead, he entered a law office in Salisbury, North Carolina. For two generations afterward, the broad and shady streets of that sleepy little town, already old when the Revolution began, rang with tales of the pranks of Andrew Jackson.

Over six feet tall now, erect, slender, he already was the recognized leader of the town—in cockfighting, horseracing, dancing, and drinking.

One night, having a good time at the old Rowan Tavern, he and his friends literally ripped the place apart. He rode a horse beautifully, ran footraces, carried off gates, and shot so well that he could get two bullets into the same hole.

"Jackson up for President? Jackson . . .?" later recalled one old lady. "Why . . . my husband would not bring him into the house. . . . Well, if Andrew Jackson can be President, anybody can."

But, for all his frolics, Jackson went at the study of law with the intensity with which he did everything else. "I was but a raw lad then," he said afterward, "but I did my best." And it was as a full-fledged attorney-at-law that young Andrew Jackson finally left Salisbury to resume its interrupted peace, and crossed over the mountains into Tennessee.

The Gentleman from Tennessee

IN THOSE DAYS, Tennessee was the Wild West. The West was certainly the place for a young man of Jackson's energy and toughness. He had known to the full the hardships of war, poverty, illness, and death. Nothing could be worse for him than what he had already endured.

Originally, Tennessee had been Washington County, North Carolina. But so troublesome had the settlers been with their loud outcries for help against the Indians, that North Carolina was quite willing to cede the whole vast area to the federal government. Enraged, the settlers had briefly set up housekeeping on their own as "the free state of Franklin." They had their own governor, "Nolichucky Jack" Sevier, a buckaroo who for sheer color of personality rivaled Jackson himself. Nashville, at the close of the eighteenth century, was a mere huddle of log shanties, clustered around old Fort Nashborough. Settlers slept on skins heaped on the floor, and the floor itself might be only rough planks laid on the earth, with snakes sometimes gliding up through the cracks.

Jackson had scarcely arrived before he was named public prosecutor or attorney-general, an "honor" not nearly so great as it seems. Law and order were unknown quantities in Nashville. Many residents had left the East suddenly and for very good reasons; killing was looked upon as murder only when the victim had had no chance for self-defense. The one lawyer in town, before Jackson arrived, had been engaged by every debtor in the community, and won his cases without opposition. Hence, any man or organization to whom money was owed was on the verge of bankruptcy.

Jackson was a good prosecutor; he knew how to win. His fervent appeals easily persuaded juries; in fact, his very intensity often made them sympathize with his usually unpopular causes. He rapidly became known in the community, but he lived outside of town with a widow, Mrs. John Donelson, and her family. There he met his landlady's daughter Rachel, pretty, brunette, bright-eyed, and twenty-two.

Five years earlier, Rachel had married a young

man of good family named Lewis Robards, and had moved into his home in Kentucky. Almost from the first, he had flown into jealous rages whenever a man looked at her. A few weeks before Jackson's arrival, Robards had ordered his wife never to show her face in his house again, and had sent her back to her mother in Tennessee.

But in the spring of 1789 Robards suddenly appeared in Nashville, eager to beg forgiveness of Rachel. For a brief time, they stayed together, but Rachel continued to make frequent visits to the home of her mother, and there Robards' suspicious eye fell upon Andrew Jackson.

The uproar was such that Jackson decided to move out, but not before he and Robards had exchanged "harmless shots" and had come dangerously near to fighting a duel. Rachel went back to Kentucky with her husband, but it was no use. The old accusations started up again. This time, Robards' jealousy reached such a peak that Mrs. Donelson—unwisely—sent Andrew Jackson to bring Rachel back to Tennessee. Later, Robards would call this an elopement. At the time, he merely followed his wife to Nashville, threatened her, and slurred Jackson.

Jackson became so angry at Robards that he threatened to "cut his ears out of his head." At

Jackson was married to Rachel Donelson Robards in 1791, under the mistaken belief that she had been legally divorced from her previous husband. In 1794, when the divorce became official, the Jacksons remarried.

this point Robards suddenly fled back into Kentucky. From the safety of his home, he threatened to return once more—and this time he would carry Rachel off by force. This was too much. Completely terrified, Rachel boarded a flatboat for Natchez, Mississippi, accompanied by an elderly man as her protector. Jackson, blaming himself for the whole mess, decided that he, too, should offer his protection, and went along on another boat.

On that long journey, what Robards had imagined and Rachel had feared and Jackson had not even dared admit to himself actually began to come true. Rachel and Jackson fell helplessly in love. News was waiting for them in Natchez: Robards had divorced his wife on the grounds of desertion. Rachel's gay vivacity dimmed. "I expected him to kill me but this is worse," she murmured. But Jackson's tender wooing soothed and comforted her, and, in August 1791, the couple were married in the tall parlor of a stately brick mansion called Springfield.

They returned to Nashville in the fall, settled down, and lived happily for two busy years. Then a shattering blow struck them. Robards had not divorced Rachel, as they had been told; he had merely applied for a divorce. Now he got one, on the grounds that Rachel and Andrew Jackson had been living as man and wife.

The couple married again immediately, of course. Then Jackson got out two pistols, polished them, and made it perfectly clear that he would use them upon anybody who dared challenge Rachel's good name. At least twice he did use them. But even that was not enough. The ugly story festered and was told over and over again, darkening the years of one of the most devoted couples in American history.

But Jackson's public life flourished. As prosecutor, he was becoming known all over the state, through the sheer impact of his personality. He was like the other men of his time, but more so; they fought; he fought harder. He never did anything halfway. He saw and dreamed what the average man saw and dreamed, but he acted upon his dreams—that was the difference.

He was a man of his time, stamped boldly in the colors of his time. He was original, not so much in his thinking as in what he did. He was no philosopher. He saw nothing wrong, for instance, in owning slaves, although he would have considered it wicked to be a cruel master to his slaves. Land, he believed, was earned not just by living on it, but by plowing it, mining it, building upon it. Therefore, he saw nothing wrong in driving the Indians off the land, for they only camped upon it. His creed was the Code of Honor, which included all varieties of self-defense, from dueling with pistols to fistfights.

His temper was violent, to be sure, but he often seemed more angry than he was, and somehow he always seemed to know just when to get mad. It was not until he had been jostled for the third time by a bully of the town that he grabbed a fence rail, gave him "the p'int in his belly," and stamped upon him. When a big fire broke out, it was Andrew Jackson who organized a bucketline. But when a drunk began giving contradictory orders, confusing the fire fighters, Jackson simply slammed a bucket down upon his head. "I take the responsibility," he would always say, especially when someone failed him.

He was "the most American of Americans—an embodied Declaration of Independence." Perhaps this is why the masses never lost their love for him, why as late as 1928, people in isolated districts in the Southern mountains were still voting for Andrew Jackson for President of the United States. He was young, western America in the flesh, a Democrat before the Democratic party was born officially. There were only Mr. Hamilton's Federalists and the anti-Federalists.

Democracy was sweeping the West, along the lines of the mountains: the Berkshires and the Green Mountains in New England, the Adirondacks and the Alleghenies and the Southern Appalachians. The frontiersmen were avowed anti-Federalists. Like John C. Calhoun's father, some had even opposed the adoption of the Constitution of the United States. "The United States offers us no protection," one of the Tennessee leaders had growled, thinking of the everpresent threats of the Indians and of land-hungry Spain.

Many of the frontiersmen did not look to George Washington as their leader. Young Andrew Jackson had even declared that the President should be impeached for signing a treaty with England which made no mention whatever of the chronic British outrage—the impressment of American seamen from American ships. The frontier's allegiance was to the author of the Declaration of Independence, long Tom Jefferson, himself from the foothills, and sowing the seeds of a new political party, as yet unborn.

Like Jefferson, the frontiersmen were interested not so much in the rights of property as in the rights of man. They did not want Alexander Hamilton's National Bank and a sound dollar, but paper money, freely circulated. They were not interested in an all-powerful national government, but in the sovereignty of the individual states. As "the free state of Franklin," the yet-to-be-named Tennessee had held out for three years as an independent, sovereign (if outlaw), power.

Yet it was inevitable that Tennessee should come into the Union now that 70,000 residents could be counted. And it was equally inevitable that Andrew Jackson should join the men meeting in Knoxville to draw up a constitution for the new state. Still in his twenties, Jackson had not sought this honor. In fact, his lifelong rule was that a good citizen should never seek an office and never decline one. But it was inevitable that he should go into politics. His gift for leadership was instinctive and unmistakable. In the end, it was he who proposed the name of Tennessee for the new American state.

The state constitution, as they drew it up, was rankly democratic. For instance, any man could vote after six months' residence. A property holder could vote after having lived in the state for but one day! Congress debated admitting Tennessee for nearly four months. It was fitting that in the last year of the presidency of George Washington, the long, lanky, redheaded man with the big nose, Tennessee should have chosen as its first Representative in the House, another long, lanky redheaded man with a big nose. Young Andrew Jackson arrived in Philadelphia, the temporary capital of the United States, in December 1796, just in time to hear George Washington deliver his last annual message to Congress. He was in time, also, to vote, along with eleven others, against a resolution of praise for Washington's Administration. This was, of course, to be expected from a frontiersman.

The cultured, classic city of Philadelphia was unimpressed, except in the negative, by young Andrew Jackson. He had arrived in frontier buckskins, his long hair tied back with the skin of an eel. The Democratic party press could blare about HAMILTON . . . PAPER MONEY . . . NATIONAL BANK, but the business of the Republic was being sedately transacted by gentlemen from Boston and Virginia, not Indian fighters from the backwoods. Jackson's actions were typical—and expected. He scorned the burying of bills in committees. He presented the petition of an Indian chief who had helped the whites on the frontier, and he voted for what would have been regarded, in later years, as a property tax—a tax upon slaves. Tennessee thrilled to his "spirited manner," but for him public life seemingly held no charms at all. He was young and homesick; he wrote to his "Dearest Heart" of his desire to be restored to her arms, and he promptly retired at the end of his term.

Code of Honor

LEISURE NEVER PLAYED ANY PART in the life of Andrew Jackson, and he was soon back in Washington again. His friend William Blount was expelled from the Senate for a "high misdemeanor," involving a plot to invade Florida and Louisiana. This was a favorite idea in the West. Tennessee had no objections whatever, but the United States Senate did, and Jackson at thirty was almost forcibly sent to Washington as Blount's successor.

He did his job, seeing to it that every man in his state who had lost property to the Indians or who had fought them had his losses made good by the federal government. Several times he arose to speak, but as the presiding officer, Vice-President Thomas Jefferson, is reputed to have observed, Jackson would become so choked with rage he could not say one word. Jefferson decided that the young Senator was a passionate, dangerous man.

But the suave, dark-eyed Senator from New York, Aaron Burr, found himself charmed by the rough young man from Tennessee. So was a youthful Representative from New York named Edward Livingston. Cultured, educated, wealthy, he was Jackson's opposite in every way. Yet a friendship sprang up between them that would mean much to the future history of the United States.

Jackson resigned from the Senate in 1798. He found it too slow-moving for his taste. He was bored with playing Senator in a red morocco chair. A seat on the bench of the Superior Courts of Tennessee was awaiting him. For the next few years he worked hard, riding hundreds of miles through the unsettled wilderness to district courts at Nashville, Knoxville, Jonesboro, and other frontier communities. He was nearly drowned crossing a stream, nearly killed by Indians, but he survived. All this was far more to his liking.

None of his decisions are on record, but the tradition goes that they were "short, untechnical, unlearned, sometimes ungrammatical, and generally right." One thing is sure: when he was not blinded by passion, his sense of justice was steady and certain, and that helped to make up for his ignorance of abstract legalities.

His salary was $600 a year—a fair amount of money for those days—but he needed it. In his years as prosecuting attorney there had often been no money to pay him, so he had taken land instead and begun to build a huge plantation. He owned a frame house called Hunter's Hill and thousands of acres of land, at a time when land was money. Now he went into business in a big way. He sent his farm produce by wagon to Nashville, then by flatboat down the Cumberland, Ohio, and Mississippi rivers. Unfortunately, a lot of his business was done on credit, and he and the people who owed him money got caught in a financial panic in 1798–99.

Jackson paid up; he hated debt. His house had to go and much of his land. He and Rachel moved back into a log cabin on what land remained; they called it The Hermitage. Now Jackson began to make money with thoroughbred racehorses. He made a long trip into Virginia to buy a famous racer called Truxton, then believed to be the finest horse in the country. He had good fighting cocks, too, and Andrew Jackson's cocks and horses usually won.

He was on his way to becoming the first man in Tennessee, but for one very real rival. This was "a prince in a hunting shirt," former Governor "Nolichucky Jack" Sevier. Sevier was past fifty now, but still erect and military-looking. He was the foremost fighting man in the state; he had led troops into thirty-five battles during the Revolution and had never received a wound. At the famed battle of King's Mountain, he had terrorized the British into thinking that his troops were regiments instead of companies. The weird and roving noise of his men's Indian-style war whoops was to be known in that later and more terrible Civil War as the Rebel yell.

Now he and young Jackson were competing for the foremost military post in Tennessee, Major-General of the state militia. Jackson emerged the winner. Coolness grew rapidly between them, and when Jackson mentioned his services, Sevier snapped back: "Services? I know of no great service you have rendered the country except taking a trip to Natchez with another man's wife."

That did it. The shooting started so quickly that one bullet hit a bystander. Jackson was shooting to kill and only the necessary reloading stopped him. Friends quickly separated the contenders, but the feud smoldered. These were "mad, fighting times." Dueling, or the Code of Honor, as it was called, was a favorite outdoor sport of the South and West. Men seldom quar-

Jackson became major general of the Tennessee militia in 1802. His stern discipline, proud bearing, and success in battle earned him the nickname "Old Hickory."

reled without bringing matters to a head—and a fight. Charleston even had a dueling club; here in the West, fingernails were grown long for the express purpose of "gouging" or digging out an opponent's eyes.

Sevier and Jackson had more words outside a courtroom, and were thereby bound by the Code to meet and "have it out," even if only with fisticuffs. When Sevier failed to show up for the fight, Jackson found him and charged him like a knight on horseback, using a cane as a spear; Sevier fell under his horse. The affair was patched up, although the bitterness lingered. Then someone else tampered with the "sacred name" of Jackson's wife.

The offender was Charles Dickinson, a hard-drinking young blade of Nashville. The first time, Jackson accepted his apology; the second time, a grim duel to the death was planned. Both men practiced, but Dickinson was the best shot in Tennessee. He hit a string with a bullet four times at twenty-four feet and left it hanging for Jackson to see. So Jackson made a grim decision. He would stand and deliberately wait for Dickinson to shoot him, then at his leisure shoot and bring him down.

It was so done. At the cry of "Fire!" Dickinson fired, straight and true, and Jackson, tall and thin in a loose coat, wavered a little but still stood. Then, deliberately, he raised and fired his own pistol. Dickinson reeled. He fell to the ground, blood pouring out of his side. Jackson mounted his horse and rode away. "I should have hit him," he said, "if he had shot me through the brain."

Outside an inn, Jackson asked a maid for buttermilk. When she brought it, he was secretly looking inside his coat, and, horrified, she saw that he was soaked with blood. "He has pinked me a little," he admitted to a friend, downed a whole quart of buttermilk, went inside the inn and gave himself over to a doctor. Later, he sent the doctor and a bottle of wine over to Dickinson, but it was too late. The man had died in agony. His only comfort was that he had been told by his friends that he had mortally wounded Jackson in the chest.

He had indeed given Jackson a serious wound dangerously close to his heart. Some believe that years afterward it was Dickinson's bullet that finally killed Andrew Jackson. Meanwhile, Jackson's popularity sank to a low ebb in Tennessee. His shooting of Dickinson seemed more like premeditated murder than a duel, and he became generally regarded as a violent and dangerous man.

In the autumn of this year of 1806, Jackson had a visitor, also the survivor of a duel which had made him an outcast in the East. Here in the West it made him a hero. In the West duels were esteemed and Alexander Hamilton was not. So as the killer of Alexander Hamilton, former Vice-President Aaron Burr was wined and dined from Virginia on west to Tennessee.

Jackson welcomed him in the newly built Hermitage, a square log dwelling of a few rooms, dominated by a huge fireplace. The house was really for Rachel's benefit; during most of the year Jackson practically lived on his horse. But his hospitality was unbounded. As for Burr—dark, dynamic, driving—no one quite knew what he was there for, perhaps not even he himself. He talked about the people surging into the great valley of the Mississippi. He talked of Spain—which everyone hated—and the coming war with Spain—which everyone expected. But he said nothing to anyone about what he was doing to bring on this war. With a hint that he had the official blessing of Washington, he talked of heading up an expedition to Texas and Mexico. And finally he vanished into the mists along the Mississippi to pursue his dream.

Disturbing rumors drifted back to Jackson as they were drifting across the rest of the country.

Once again the talk was of the Spanish plot; Burr had evidently fallen victim to the old dream which had tempted empire builders since Alexander Hamilton—to seize the Spanish-owned territories west of Louisiana and southward to Texas, Mexico, and Cuba and annex them to the United States. But was Aaron Burr seeking only to widen the American horizons, or was he engaged in some mad adventure of his own? It was said that New Orleans, not Texas, was his immediate goal, that he planned to detach the newly organized Louisiana Territory from the United States and set up a separate confederacy. One of his ardent young supporters visited the Hermitage and spoke wildly of his friend's plan to "divide the Union." Genuinely alarmed, Jackson knew what he had to do.

He wrote a secret note to Governor William C. Claiborne of Louisiana, warning of a possible *"attack from quarters you do not . . . suspect."* New Orleans should be readied for action. "And beware of an attack as well from our own country as from Spain. . . . I will die . . . before I would . . . see the Union disunited." To President Jefferson he personally wrote that in event of attack "FROM ANY QUARTER," he would volunteer his services, along with militia troops under his command as Major-General of Tennessee.

The War Department hesitated. Word had gotten around in Washington that Jackson was in league with the conspirators, and Jackson, indignant, sneered that the Secretary of War was "not fit for a granny." Meanwhile, Jefferson issued a proclamation denouncing Burr as a traitor. Shortly afterward, the former Vice-President was picked up and arrested, and Andrew Jackson was summoned to Richmond to appear as a state's witness at his trial.

But Jackson was not yet sure "that treason was . . . intended by Burr," although, "if ever it was," he should be hanged. What he was sure about was that the commanding American general at New Orleans, James Wilkinson (whom we now know to have been an agent in the pay of Spain), "went hand in hand" with Burr, then denounced him to save his own skin. "If Burr is guilty," Jackson wrote, "Wilkinson has participated in the treason."

Of what was Burr guilty? Dreaming of an empire? Hamilton had done this, and Sam Houston was later to turn the dream into reality. Jackson shrewdly suspected that Burr was guilty of being popular, of being a disruptive influence in the Jefferson Administration. Some way had to be found to get rid of him; was not this perhaps the real purpose of the trial? If so, it succeeded. The trial tarnished Burr's name, although it failed to prove him guilty. And the unfairness of it made Andrew Jackson sick, to the point where he went out on the street and denounced the trial and Mr. Jefferson and was hastily excused and taken off the list of witnesses. Another dark mark was written against his name in Washington.

4

War: Public and Private

MEANWHILE, BATTLES WERE BREWING of a quite different kind. The War of 1812 had been "inevitable" for more than a decade, with first Adams and then Jefferson playing for time. But in the West there was a very real question as to who the enemy was going to be. Would it be Spain, with whom the young Federal Union shared an uneasy peace and blurred territorial boundary lines, beginning and ending no one quite knew where? Or if, as Andrew Jackson had long been convinced, "We must fight England again," would not the new West stand to gain more as an outright ally of Spain? Of what use was it to rely on a Union so-called, that thus far had offered almost no protection against what many believed to be England's dream of reconquering her former territories, or against the Indians, the everpresent terror of the frontier.

War with England was declared officially in June 1812. But for the East, the real war had begun on that grim day five years earlier when the British man-of-war *Leopard* had raked the American frigate *Chesapeake* with fire, carried off four men into imprisonment and left twenty-one others dead or wounded.

As for the West, the war had begun on the Tippecanoe River in Indiana in November 1811, when 188 of the white troops, under the command of General William Henry Harrison, had fallen victim to the Indians. Years later, this affray, trumped up as a great victory, was to make "Old Tip" President of the United States. At the time, the "victory" was something less than glorious. The American casualties were far heavier than those of the Indians, and although the Indians temporarily withdrew, the clash brought about what the Americans most feared—an Indian-British alliance.

WAR! WAR! WAR! . . . BRITISH SAVAGE WAR. THE BLOW IS STRUCK, roared the headlines in the West. In the West, at least, there was no doubt as to who the real enemy was. At least ninety guns taken from the Indians were new and of English manufacture. The Indians were massing along the frontier, and, whether officially or unofficially, they were armed with British weapons. This was a crime that could be neither forgiven nor forgotten—and in the West, at least, there was no doubt, no hesitation. The Indians must be put down, their source of supply wiped out, and Canada seized. The United States would have to fight England again.

Jackson had been aware of this years before. Grimly, he had concluded that Mr. Jefferson was about the best President "in theory and the worst in practice" that it was possible to imagine. Jackson looked beyond the frontier; he knew that what was coming was more than an Indian war. How long was his country to be kicked and cuffed around at His Majesty's pleasure, American sailors to be ripped off the decks of their own ships? War was coming. Andrew Jackson was ready for it and eager for it. He only hoped it would come before he was too old to fight.

The Army, it seemed, did not share Jackson's enthusiasm. Jackson had sent word to the War Department that he would raise 2500 men, seize Quebec within ninety days, and take Canada. Instead, the one Major-General of militia who was ready and eager to fight was left to plow his fields in Tennessee. In the Washington city of Jefferson and Madison, it was no help that discredited Aaron Burr was pleading that Andrew Jackson be given a commission. "I'll tell you why they don't employ Jackson," Burr told a rising young politician by the name of Martin Van Buren. "It's because he is a friend of mine." (Jackson was no longer Burr's friend, but he was thought to be.)

The terrified Americans who, at the beginning of the war, actually marched up into Canada and back again were completely unready to fight. The generals were the same way. From the first, the conflict went badly. Old England was invading, New England was on the verge of seceding, and every time a battle loomed, the Americans ran away. Both the generals and the men seemed to have but a single idea—to surrender. All hope of Canada was lost; Detroit was lost; the whole Northwest was lost. . . . "The news . . . almost killed me," Jackson confessed.

Although he was passed over for command of the troops on the western frontier, Jackson did get into the war finally, by the back door. Late in 1813, the Governor of Tennessee was called upon to supply troops to reinforce General Wilkinson, still in command in New Orleans, as a reward for having testified against Aaron Burr. With Michigan firmly in British hands, Wilkinson had become convinced of a new and not entirely impossible danger. Should the British, he reasoned, mass their fleets at New Orleans, then sweep up the Mississippi and join their forces to the northward, conditions in the West would be very unpleasant indeed.

The War Department agreed, and a belated call went out to Jackson. Jackson was ready, although he packed his dueling pistols in case of a personal "meeting" with Wilkinson.

The Tennessee volunteers assembled. It was bitter winter weather, with snow lying deep on the ground. On January 7th, they began to move: "Down the Cumberland to the Ohio; down the Ohio to the Mississippi; down the Mississippi; toward New Orleans"—500 miles in twenty-one days!

At Natchez there was word from Wilkinson. He was not ready; the supplies were not ready; the war itself was not ready. The British invasion of New Orleans, as it turned out, was more than a year away. The Tennessee volunteers waited. And waited. Then came a letter from the War Department, dated February 6th, 1813, and Jackson blew up with a roar.

He was informed that the emergency was over, the troops no longer required. They were to be dismissed. The President wanted to express his thanks to everybody.

Dismissed! Five hundred miles from home—with the war still raging! Jackson raged too, but a young officer named Thomas Hart Benton persuaded him to tone down his "violently insubordinate" letter to the War Department.

The volunteers had had to supply their own arms and blankets and homespun hunting shirts of blue or brown. Now their clothes and shoes were worn out and there was no food. Grimly, Jackson sent Benton on to Washington to collect money for the necessary supplies and pledged his own credit to the merchants of Natchez. Only then would he begin the long march home. And as he moved among his men, surprisingly gentle and patient and fatherly, giving his own horse to a sick soldier, sharing and enduring all that his men endured, some one called him "Old Hickory." He was as tough, they said, as hickory wood. The name stuck.

Back home new trouble awaited him. Tom Benton's brother Jesse had unfortunately involved himself in a quarrel with a friend of Jackson's; the friend asked Jackson to be his second in a duel. Unwisely, and reluctantly, Jackson agreed. Unfortunately, Jesse Benton fired and then stooped over at just the wrong moment. He got a bullet in a place that made it impossible for him to sit down for a long time. Everybody thought this was very funny, except the enraged Jesse and his brother Tom, back from Washington with Jackson's money. Tom was furious that Jackson had acted as a second and denounced him in such language that the General swore he would horsewhip Tom Benton on sight.

They met in a hallway of the quaint, rambling City Hotel in Nashville. Tom fumbled for a gun; Jackson whipped out a pistol and backed him down the hall onto the veranda. Suddenly, from Jackson's rear, Jesse Benton fired, and Jackson fell. A moment later Tom tumbled backwards down a whole flight of stairs, his own gun spinning after him.

Jackson's shoulder was shattered. "I'll keep my arm," he muttered, as the surgeons tried to stem the bleeding. Public opinion veered to his side now, and, claiming that he was hounded by "Jackson's puppies," Tom Benton left Tennessee for Missouri. Meanwhile, with Jackson flat on his back and too weak to move, the call went out for the "brave and patriotic General" again to lead the troops of Tennessee.

It was a two-front war now. The Creek Indians were on the march in a desperate, last-ditch fight for survival. Their great chief, the "graceful and majestic" Tecumseh, had dreamed of uniting all tribes from Florida to the Great Lakes, sweeping the whites into the sea. Tecumseh was dead now, but his dream lived on. It was a threat and a challenge to the white man's belief that God had meant the good earth for those who could best use it, and that it was part of the divine plan for them to help God along.

The whites resented and feared the Indians, resented their camping and hunting on rich bottom land obviously intended for corn. They feared men who carried red sticks and painted their faces black and stuck eagle plumes on their heads. It was fear of Indians—British-led Indians —fear of mutilation and scalping and torture— that brought on the panic which caused the troops to run in Canada. It was fear now—in the broiling heat of August 1813—that brought more than 500 settlers to a flat, swampy region of Alabama where rose a log stockade known as Fort Mims.

Alabama was then part of Mississippi Territory. For weeks, raids and rumors had rippled across the land—then silence. The hot days dragged. The door of the fortress yawned open. Children were playing outside and women cooking dinner within, when the cry of *"Indians! Indians!"* sounded.

They could not close the gate. Indians with tomahawks burst in, howling and dancing. Burning arrows turned the fortress and buildings into a "roaring sea of flame." Children were swung up by the feet "and their brains dashed out." People were trampled to death; "women were cut to pieces." Twelve persons escaped, but not a white woman or child was left alive.

Not ten days later, arriving to bury the dead, the Army found the sky black with buzzards. Dogs were chewing on the scalped and mutilated bodies.

All over Alabama, families fled like sheep to stockades. And after them, more Indians swept scythelike across the deserted farms, burning and stealing. For a time, it looked as though all the white settlers might be wiped out.

5

Redcoats and Redskins

IT WAS THIRTY-ONE DAYS before the news of the Fort Mims massacre reached New York. But already the call for help had gone out to Tennessee and to Andrew Jackson, who, gritting his teeth against pain, assured the War Department that his health was completely restored. A month after his meeting with the Benton brothers, Jackson was helped on to his horse. His arm was in a sling. He could not wear a sleeve or bear the weight of an epaulette, and any sudden move or twist sent agony through his body, but his calls to action breathed energy and fire. His men would "revenge the cruelties." They must not be shaken by the "hideous yells" of the enemy; bayonets, not yells, would determine the outcome. "Soldiers, the order for a charge will be the signal for victory."

He had 2500 men, including Davy Crockett

with his rifle and hunting shirt and tall stories. The weather was beautiful; spirits were high, and, in their enthusiasm, the men marched thirty-two miles in one day.

But Jackson was grim. "There is an enemy whom I dread much more than I do the hostile Creeks . . . Famine," he wrote. The problem was to march through a pathless wilderness and find there waiting every week, a thousand bushels of grain, twenty tons of meat, gallons and gallons of whiskey—in short, ten wagon-loads of food. Naturally, none of these supplies could get through. There was no food ahead, but there were Indians. There was no food at camp, so Jackson sent out foraging parties and plunged further into the wilderness.

A detachment of his men under General John Coffee clashed with the Creeks and killed over 300 of them. Six days later, Jackson again beat the Creeks, but soon after that, the hungry men had had enough and wanted to go home. Jackson's own running battle was against mutiny. When the militia revolted, he blocked their path with the volunteers; when the volunteers revolted, he blocked their way with the militia. After that, this particular joke wore thin—and so did the men. No food came. Jackson begged his hungry forces to wait just two more days. They did, then started back for Tennessee.

On their way, they met the promised beef cattle, slaughtered and ate them. Then, "filled with beef and valor," they refused to return to fight. Jackson galloped ahead, ordered General Coffee to fire on any deserter, then followed up with volleys of oaths. He raved and he swore. "His blue eyes blazed fire." He seized a musket and promised to shoot down the first man who moved. They stood, sullen and silent, and finally broke ranks and returned. The man whose gun had been borrowed suddenly burst out: "Why General, that gun ain't loaded—not even primed."

Despite Jackson's bitter sneers at "fireside patriots," the men had a legal technicality on their side. Many had signed up for a year, or twelve months from the date of enlistment. Jackson declared a year to be 365 days of *active service* in the field. Jackson had no interest in legalities or technicalities. So long as there was a war to be fought, he would do what had to be done despite orders that came too late, or never arrived at all.

More troops were brought up. Again they clashed with the Creeks, killing about 200 of them in a victory whose reverberations echoed back East, which had been scarcely aware there was an

Indian war at all. Accounts appeared in a few newspapers. A question was being asked: "Who is this General Jackson?"

Tennessee Volunteers began to swarm to Jackson's colors. Among them was a hapless boy of 18, named John Woods, who had threatened an officer with a gun. Jackson's patience snapped; an example had to be made. "A fellow has mutinied," he said, "and will have to be shot." Woods was duly executed. Jackson spent two sleepless nights, but once the execution was carried out, there was no further talk of mutiny.

In central Alabama, a heavily wooded peninsula of about a hundred acres reached like a horseshoe into the bend of the Tallapoosa river. This was "the heart of the Creek country." Here the Indians had built a fortress of logs, pierced with holes through which they could fire, and backed with a mass of brushwood. Nearby floated canoes ready for retreat into the wilderness of swamp and forest. If the fortress was carried, there was always the river. But Jackson, after the army's eleven-day march, cutting roads and pushing boats through fifty-five miles of unbroken country, was convinced that the Indians "had penned themselves up for slaughter."

It so proved. The 39th Regiment marched straight to the breastworks and exchanged shot "muzzle to muzzle" with the Indians through the portholes. Fierce hand-to-hand fighting broke out. Like ants fleeing from a hill, the Indians dove into the river, their dark heads vanishing under pools of blood. None would surrender.

Scaling the breastworks, stalwart young Sam Houston of the 39th fell with a barbed arrow in his abdomen. When it was pulled out, a gush of blood came with it. Jackson ordered him to the rear, but when cannon were dragged up and the call for a charge sounded, it was Houston who led the way, until he was pinned to the ground with two bullets in his shoulder. In "extremest agony," the hero of the day lay untended all night on the damp ground. The surgeon said that he would die anyway, and it was no use torturing him by dressing his wounds. Incredibly, somehow he lived.

Gradually, the "slow, laborious slaughter" came to an end. Fire blazed in the logs and the underbrush. With the troops mopping up by twos and threes, the fighting dwindled to a standstill. More than 750 Creeks had been killed and only some 50 Americans. Not only were the Creeks broken at Horseshoe Bend, but also the fighting power of the red man in Eastern North America was virtually ended.

The advancing Americans found the Indian villages abandoned; the enemy had vanished. However, the noble leader of the Creeks, William Weatherford, did come to report that, with their fields and villages laid waste, the Creek women and children were starving in the woods. "Kill him," shouted the troops.

Jackson silenced them. "Any man who would kill a man as brave as this would rob the dead," he said. For most of the summer of 1814, 5000 Creeks drew their food from federal supplies.

However, this was Jackson's only act of mercy toward the Indians. The dream of Tecumseh, he was determined, had to be shattered. The road to New Orleans was now open from Tennessee, and what had been Indian country had been made "safe as the lawn of the Hermitage." Now the state militias could be freed for the bigger war with the British Redcoats.

Empowered to make peace, the General dictated the terms of the harsh Treaty of Fort Jackson to a conquered people, their chiefs ranged before him, silent and sullen and "fantastically garbed." Although he left the Indians 150,000 square miles of their "country," far from the white settlements, he demanded and got a tremendous cession of territory that came to be the greatest cotton-growing sector of the United States. This was the price the Creeks had to pay for having waged war at all.

Meanwhile, in the House of Representatives in Washington, a petition was being circulated for a commission in the regular Army for Andrew Jackson. Here in this war of disasters was one successful military campaign. Here was a general who could fight. Just at this time, General William Henry Harrison, hero of the battle of Tippecanoe, and the only other fighting general, resigned after an argument with the Secretary of War. On May 31, 1814, Jackson was appointed in his place as a Major-General in the Army of the United States. Orders went out to him swiftly: the British were threatening; the Gulf Coast was imperiled. The campaign for New Orleans was underway.

Jackson's victory had been great, but he paid for it. His health was wrecked from the wretched food and exposure, and he was never a well man again. Chronic diarrhea wracked him. Dickinson's bullet irritated his lung. Hideous attacks of pain goaded his temper to the breaking point. Any lesser man would have gone home, but not Andrew Jackson.

It was the low, dark ebb of the war for the

United States. Washington had been invaded and burned. The London *Times* called President Madison "this fellow . . . notorious for . . . barbarous warfare." A great British fleet of fifty ships was fitting out at Jamaica and the British even sent unofficial word to the citizens of New Orleans that it was on its way. Edward Livingston former Congressman from New York, and now a resident of New Orleans, had organized a Committee of Defense. The legislature had done nothing but fight with the Governor, nothing to defend the city. Meanwhile, the British were using the moldering, sleepy old Spanish town of Pensacola as a base, and His Majesty's ships floated comfortably in the harbor, under the protection of Fort Barrancas.

Looking upon a new and shining musket that had been captured from a Creek, Jackson had dramatic proof of what he knew already. Not only were the British allied with Spain, but still more Indians were being enlisted to serve under the colors of the King. Jackson knew what he had to do.

He wrote the War Department that if he could only seize the ships, "reduce" Pensacola, and battle the British and the Indians right there in Florida, the war in the South would be over. The

War Department agreed, but his official orders did not arrive until six months later. Then the war was over.

Meanwhile, Jackson had to move on his own. With new volunteers swinging down the roads from Tennessee, and the hulls of four British ships lying just over the horizon off Mobile, Jackson's men entrenched themselves there at Fort Bowyer. Soon the British attacked. The Americans' 20- and 24-pound guns raked the British ships with fire. One was sunk, another crippled, another set ablaze. Night fell, but back in Mobile Jackson heard the explosions and mistakenly thought that the British had managed to blow up his fort. Instead the Americans had won a clearcut victory as the remaining British forces withdrew.

Where would they strike next? Jackson was sure it would be New Orleans, but he was equally sure of something else. So long as the British held Pensacola, the whole Gulf Coast was unsafe. He must throw the enemy out. Meanwhile, he was waiting for men, and he had to wait six intolerable weeks. At the same time, the three months' men threatened mutiny, and "went off rioting." Jackson had had enough. With the full authority now of a regular officer, he prosecuted; 200 men were arrested and court-martialed.

Haggard and pale and often prostrate with pain, Jackson suddenly moved like a daredevil. While the fight lasted there was no tiring him. Without orders, he struck at Pensacola. His men stormed and captured the city, forced the British to abandon and blow up Fort Barrancas at the harbor mouth, and were back in Mobile in seven days' time. Not one man was lost. But the reverberations from abroad were as explosive as the shell fire. Although Jackson had politely requested the Spanish Governor to surrender the city before Jackson marched into it, the official protests from Spain spoke of wanton and brutal outrages. And the ravaged and invaded United States thrilled. Here indeed was a general who could fight.

6

Victory at New Orleans

THE BIGGEST CAMPAIGN OF ALL loomed ahead of him. On December 1, 1814, Jackson and his men reached New Orleans. The residents viewed the newcomers with no great enthusiasm. New Orleans was hardly yet an American city. Scarcely twelve years had passed since the tri-color of Napoleon's France had slid down a pole in the central square, and the Stars and Stripes had risen jerkily, only to stick halfway, as the crowd howled with glee. A few years earlier it had been the flag of Spain that had flown over New Orleans and before that the lilies of the old French monarchy. New Orleans was indeed the nation's melting pot, containing some Americans of uncertain background, the native French-Spanish Creoles, blacks, free and slave, and "rascals of all nations." Small wonder that the Governor of Louisiana had warned Jackson that any "ardent zeal" for the American cause was lacking. If New Orleans were to be defended, it would have to be defended from the outside.

Jackson called for a military review. The notes of the French *Marseillaise* sounded through the pouring rain. The gorgeous reds and greens, blues and golds of the smart uniforms of the New Orleans Creole companies contrasted violently with the long shabby men with the long rifles and the coonskin caps. "Dirty Shirts," the citizens called them. Their hawkeyed commander, worn to a skeleton, and wearing a threadbare uniform and unblacked boots, looked "more fit for the hospital than the field."

Yet one glance from the gaunt man with the blazing blue eyes and soldiers tingled and felt the impact of greatness. That evening, at a dinner given by Mrs. Edward Livingston, the power of Jackson's magnetism was so great it was as if there was no one else in the room. For this occasion, "erect, composed," his prematurely white hair a startling contrast to his sun-bronzed skin, Jackson wore a clean, new, blue uniform and polished boots, and bowed with grace and charm over the hands of the ladies. A backwoodsman? inquired one. "Why, Madame, he is a prince!"

He had little time for social affairs. The military situation alone concerned him. New Orleans was a prize. Over a million dollars' worth of cotton was stored here and ten thousand hogsheads of sugar and a fleet of boats. Militarily, the problem was the Mississippi, "two hundred rivers in one." Water was as much above the city as below it; fog, murk and mist veiled swamps and inlets, until pushed aside by sudden gusts of wind. True this might provide cover for defense. But Jackson was all too well aware that there was no telling by which one of six possible routes the British might enter and bear down upon the city.

New Orleans shook with the General's energy; some even compared him to that driving demon, Napoleon. Although he was often too weak to stand, unable to eat, and had no time to sleep, it was as if a miracle were keeping him alive. He assigned every man a job—ordered every bayou to be obstructed by logs and earth, and guards to be posted. Never did he doubt that he would hurl the British back, yet none knew better than he the odds against him.

He had about 2000 men on hand, plus 4000 more a week's march away, eight small boats, and a few regular troops manning fortifications. He had also received—and accepted—an offer of help from a strange source: a free-booter and buccaneer named Jean LaFitte. This patriotic pirate held command of a large body of men encamped in the bayous below the city. The Governor had offered $500 for LaFitte's arrest; LaFitte had offered $1500 for the capture of the Governor. He had also turned down an offer of $30,000 in cash from the British to join their service. Now he turned himself over to Jackson, price on his head and all.

The British forces—including 21,000 sailors, marines, and fighting men—were on their way. Their fleet included the 74-gun *Royal Oak* and Admiral Sir Alexander Cochrane's flagship, the *Tonnant*, taken from the French by Lord Nelson at the Battle of the Nile. Others were commanded by Nelson's old captains, Hardy and Troubridge. The ships were "gay with flags and alive with red uniforms." Anticipation—and hopes—were high. For aboard were the men who had burned Washington, who had fought with Wellington and defeated Napoleon.

On December 14 news reached New Orleans that a British squadron had entered Lake Borgne; by controlling these waters, the enemy would be able to maneuver at will within a few miles of the city. Terror gripped the residents but Jackson responded by an immediate declaration of martial law. He issued his orders immediately, scouring the streets for men and the cellars and attics for old weapons, anything that would fire, for many of his Tennessee volunteers had only hunting knives, spades, or pickaxes.

Every man was drafted into his motley army: merchants, lawyers, freemen, Choctaw Indians. All were sent out to dig breastworks and hoist cannons, planters beside their slaves. Many labored grumbling, for it was known that Jackson had decided to set the city on fire rather than let it fall to the British.

Along the streets emptied of men, the women and children were crying. Jackson reassured them with this pledge: "I will smash them." He ate four tablespoonfuls of rice and lay down to sleep, his only sleep in seventy hours.

On the 23rd more bad news arrived. The British had found a secret route from Lake Borgne; and there were now 5000 first-class troops encamped on the grounds of the Villere plantation, a scant eight miles below the city.

Old Hickory acted with customary speed and decision. By sunset he had 2000 troops facing the British. When darkness came, he floated a small merchant ship that had been fitted with cannon silently down the Mississippi to a position opposite the British lines. Its guns boomed. This opening salvo signaled the beginning of two hours of chaos. The British replied with a blaze of rockets, and the night was filled with confused skirmishes.

At 9:00 P.M. Jackson retired to a prepared position along the Rodriguez Canal. He had lost 24 of his men, but the British casualties were twice as great.

The line of battle was drawn like a pencil mark across a wide plain four miles below New Orleans. The old Rodriguez Canal was a damp and grass-grown ditch, some four feet deep and twenty feet wide. Before it stretched a broad field of sugarcane stubble, framed on the left by cypress swamp and on the right by the levee of the Mississippi.

On Christmas Eve in faraway Ghent, Belgium, a treaty of peace was signed between the British and the Americans. But there was no peace in New Orleans. The Americans spent Christmas fortifying their lines. The ground was low and soggy, and the weather cold and rainy. It was no time for merrymaking.

But rumor—that his forces were at least twice the size they were—was in Jackson's favor. For it was not until this grim Christmas night that his mile-long line of defense works, thirty yards to the rear of the canal, was actually completed and cannon mounted. Constructed partly of mud and, at one end, of cut logs, the defenses rose three and four feet high and reached deep into the cypress woods. Here, it was thought, the British would make their real attack. But there was still no sign of the enemy. Cotton bales and sugar hogsheads were dragged up for bulwarks, and men dug a ditch in front of the fortifications. Jackson rode up and down the line, peering through a glass and cheering the men on. For five days and four nights he had scarcely slept and had eaten on horseback.

The morning of the 28th dawned bright and clear. Now for the first time the Americans saw the British massed in formation, "a solid column of red, their bright muskets catching the sun." The Americans greeted the sight with a "relentless cannonade." Holes opened in the red mass. The British withdrew behind their defenses.

On the 29th Jackson's men raised new batteries and cannon. Sharpshooters in "dusky brown homespun" slunk through the woods and continued to pick off hapless Britishers. New Year's Day, 1815, brought fog and the so-called "Battle of the Batteries" got under way. Thirty pieces of cannon opened fire from the British side and the American ranks split. But they returned the fire, and by noon the British efforts had slacked off. When the mist and smoke finally lifted, it revealed the British batteries "totally destroyed... formless masses of soil and broken guns." The British had lost 70 men, the Americans 34.

On January 4, 2250 Kentuckians tramped into New Orleans and shivered through the streets, holding their miserable rags together. One man in three had a tent, a blanket, or a gun; a single cooking kettle served eighty men. Again Jackson ransacked the warehouses and pled for the guns that never arrived until the fighting was over. He had to make do with what he had.

He smelled out a British plan to send men to grab the Americans' cannons and turn them against themselves. So Jackson mounted eight batteries. His embankment was now in some places twenty feet high and in others only eight. No single part of the American line could have held against the united force of the British. But with strong support in the rear, he could beat them off.

The British sensed this. Bitterly one colonel declared: "My regiment has been ordered to execution. Their dead bodies are to be used as a bridge for the rest of the army to march over."

At 1 A.M. on the morning of January 8th, Jackson roused himself and looked at his watch. "Gentlemen," he said, "we have slept enough." Gaunt and gray, he rode along his defenses, in-

Major General Jackson's defeat of the British at the Battle of New Orleans (1815) made him a national hero and launched his career in national politics.

specting and encouraging the troops. At six o'clock a British rocket soared against the sky; it was the signal for attack. Sullenly, the guns thudded into the dark. Gradually, dawn paled the sky, and the fog shifted, lifted, revealing the massed red coats, covering two thirds of the frost-white plain.

Cannonballs from the batteries ripped openings in the red columns. Stolidly, the British closed ranks and moved on. They advanced relentlessly. Shot began "cutting great lanes" in their columns, tossing aside men and pieces of men. They moved on. It was one of the last great charges in history, to rank perhaps with Pickett's doomed march across the wheat field at Gettysburg in 1863, the flood tide of the Southern Confederacy.

On they came, moving finally to within 200 yards of the range of the American rifles. The Americans held their fire tautly, as if one man, one machine—this medley of slaves and Indians, Creoles and backwoodsmen, Jean LaFitte's pirates and even a few old soldiers of Napoleon, who had faced Wellington's men before. Suddenly the cry sounded: "Fire!"

It was as if the whole embankment had burst into flame, with "a rolling, bursting, echoing noise." The American command had ordered the men to aim for the V of the Britishers' white crossbelts. They were also ordered to fire in relays, to make the invaders think they had some strange new kind of reloading gun. Over all sounded the voice of Jackson: "Stand to your guns. . . . See that every shot tells. . . . See that every shot tells. . . . Give it to them, boys. Let us finish the business today."

Half the British force had fallen now. Yet, still they moved on. Some broke and fled. Their officers rode straight into a storm of bullets, driving the men on, then fell beside them. A few brave souls jumped into the ditch and tried to claw their way up the American ramparts. Bullets tore them down.

"Fire!" Now came the Scottish Highlanders, their bagpipes wailing, their plaid kilts swinging, their bayonets gleaming. "Fire!" Two hundred more men went down level with the plain.

The Highlanders pressed on. For a moment they halted and stood unmoving, "a huge and glittering target." Then they began to fall. Five hundred of them had fallen, and others had fled or dropped into ditches, before the survivors began to retire to the sound of American cheering. Their bagpipes were still now, their young pipers dead. "Two leading regiments had vanished as if the earth had swallowed them up."

Now a company of West Indians carrying scaling ladders emerged from the mist. They saw the red blaze of fire and "dropped on their faces." Most of them were "cut to pieces."

By eight in the morning it was all over. Somberly, Jackson walked from end to end of the line. Then he gave the order to cease fire, although the batteries muttered off and on for six hours afterward.

Even he was appalled by the magnitude of his victory. The smoke slowly lifted and he saw the receding red line, the white shoulderbelts of the dead and those hiding beneath the dead. Jackson always said afterwards that he had a weird idea of the Resurrection, as hundreds who had been merely wounded or "paralyzed by fear" arose from the heaps of dead and walked over to give themselves up as prisoners. As for his men, the grimy, long-haired frontiersmen shuddered at the havoc they had wrought: 291 dead, including two generals—Pakenham and Gibbs, over 1200 wounded. The Americans had 13 dead and 39 wounded men.

The battle of New Orleans was over. There were wounded to be cared for, and the stench of the dead and hastily buried bodies would linger horribly over the field into the next summer. An isolated British force across the river had won a minor skirmish with the Americans during and after the major battle. So the British were allowed to retreat to their ships, for Jackson refused to risk committing his troops further afield. The city had been saved, and Livingston pleaded that there be no more killing. The Battle of New Orleans had been won.

The news reached Washington in the darkest hours of the war. Fear of that mighty British fleet, lurking off New Orleans ready to strike, hung heavily over the blackened ruins of the city. In Hartford, Connecticut, a group of rebellious New Englanders were holding a convention. Fiercely, they vowed to pay no more taxes for the support of the war, hinted even that they might dissolve the Union itself.

The National Intelligencer ran a headline: ALMOST INCREDIBLE VICTORY. Overnight, it was as if the sky were blazing with rockets and the name of Jackson shining from the stars. The triumph was so great that news of the actual signing of the Treaty of Ghent came as an anticlimax, and it mattered not at all that the victory was won three weeks after the war was over!

For this was victory with honor. Jackson was now a national hero. When Rachel joined him in New Orleans, bonfires to his glory were blazing all along the Mississippi Valley—the Valley along which she had fled so many years ago. Parades were marching and cannon booming, all the way to New England. The President gave the General a gold medal; every state in the Union officially expressed its thanks. And there in New Orleans to share in the triumph at the Grand Ball was Rachel Jackson. She was "the backwoods incarnate," with her calloused hands and sunbrowned skin, so dumpy and fat that the Creole ladies sneered: "She shows how far the skin can be stretched."

Rachel had the humility and good sense to ask Cora Livingston for help, and Mrs. Livingston had the kindness to give it. She could not make Rachel a great lady, of course. But she could help her buy the right clothes, and she gave parties where the women who had admired Jackson's simple and good manners could also respond to his loyal, warmhearted wife. At the ball, Jackson's admiring eyes showed clearly that to him Rachel was the most beautiful woman there. The couple won their way completely into the hearts of New Orleans society when they offered to provide some entertainment, and the skeleton-like figure of the General and the dumpling figure of Rachel bobbed wildly up and down to the country tune of "Possum Up de Gum Tree." Their seven-year-old adopted son Andrew, Jr., was also the pet of the community, Jackson often holding him in his arms while he did business, and once bringing him in his nightgown to a window to wave to the cheering crowds.

But all was not peace, especially in New Orleans. Until he was officially informed that the war was over, Jackson kept the city clamped under martial law. When a judge issued a writ of habeas corpus, he highhandedly placed his Honor under arrest, then later appeared in court to pay that same judge a $1000 fine for contempt. Then out of Mobile seeped news that shocked the country. There, before a "great concourse" of people, six blindfolded men knelt on six coffins and were shot by a firing squad. The charge had been mutiny; these were the ringleaders of the 200 militia men who were court-martialed. The rest had had their heads shaved, and were drummed out of camp. Jackson and the Governor of Tennessee had called them to six months' service; they had cited an old law setting three months as the limit. But Jackson had had enough of mutiny. Were these men spared, he was convinced, the whole army would be clamoring for release, and he was not then sure that the war was over.

7

The Democratic Candidate

BUT SOON IT WAS TIME for the victorious General to go home. He could have had the freedom of every city in America if he desired it, but his only wish was for the peace and quiet of the Hermitage, for he was in a state of near physical collapse. The celebrations for "the hero of New Orleans" could wait; months later, a necessary trip to Washington became a triumphal promenade. Even the aging Jefferson toasted the wild man from Tennessee at a huge reception in Lynchburg, although it is worthy of note that he did not entertain the General at Monticello.

In any event, Jackson had a few quiet months at home. Slowly, he began to feel better, and to enjoy again the plantation life from which he was seized so often. There were mornings in his easy chair with a youngster wedged on each side of him and another in his lap fighting with the

In 1804, Jackson bought a plantation near Nashville, Tennessee, where he built his home in 1819. Known as the Hermitage, this stately mansion was his frequent retreat and final resting place.

newspapers; race day, with a 200-foot table set up in the yard surrounded by people, roaring with a "tornado of horsetalk," Rachel interrupting a wildly profane story to say: "Mr. Jackson, will you ask a blessing?" (He did.) Then there were the long, leisurely evenings around the fire, with the young people singing Scottish airs and he and Rachel puffing on long clay pipes.

These young people were a continually changing lot. Although only Andrew Jackson, Jr., one of twins born to the frail wife of Rachel's brother, was officially adopted, at least five others were raised as Rachel and Jackson's own. His thwarted desire for fatherhood had found outlet at last. At different times the household included: John and Andrew Jackson Donelson, sons of Rachel's dead brother; William Smith, a pathetic little boy born to elderly parents who did not want him; Lincoyer, an Indian waif whom Jackson had discovered and brought home after a raid had wiped out his parents; and Andrew Jackson Hutchings, the young son of a dead law partner. In addition, the Jacksons were official guardians to two families of Butler children, whose father was dead, and the General aided in their education. All the children to him, he said, "appeared as my own."

Rachel was ever devoted, ever loyal, but all her girlish gaiety was gone. She was racked with unreasoning fears, both for herself and her husband, as a typical letter on display at the Hermitage reveals. She clung to Jackson like a child, was tormented when he left her, either for public life or the battlefield. And somehow, half-unconsciously, protesting his eagerness to be home, Jackson seized at every chance of escape. Something was driving him, goading him on.

He loved her, of course, devotedly; the man who was the terror of the Army camp and later of official Washington was never impatient with his wife or children. He was, in fact, the "gentlest and tenderest of men." Never would he have admitted, even to himself, how Rachel's almost hysterical overprotectiveness must have irked him. Yet after viewing one of Jackson's partings from his emotional wife, a friend wrote a strange paragraph, which could easily have been applied to Abraham Lincoln: "History will never record how many men have performed great deeds because they were driven out of their homes by some unbearable trait of their wives . . ."

His new call to duty came in 1817. Again, the Seminoles were making trouble along the Florida-Georgia border. So in February of the next year, it was boots and saddle and the old uniform for the General. And again, Jackson's actions were direct, dramatic, and dangerous, so much so that

Secretary of State John Quincy Adams trembled every time news arrived from the battlefield.

Three peoples—the Indians, the Spaniards, and the Americans—were grappling for the possession of East and West Florida. To Jackson it was clear that the Indians were being egged on by the Spaniards, and if the border was ever to be safe, the whole Florida territory must become American. How could this be done without officially involving the United States? Jackson had a plan; the President could let him know through informal word to a friendly Tennessee congressman. "Let it be signified to me through any channel, (say Mr. J. Rhea) that the possession of the Floridas would be desirable . . . and in sixty days it will be accomplished." (As it turned out, the job was accomplished in forty-eight days.) Monroe, however, never remembered seeing the letter. As he was ill at the time, it was "laid aside," and turned up later on. Jackson meanwhile acted upon Secretary of War Calhoun's instructions to take "the necessary measures to terminate the conflict."

"I hesitated no longer," he said afterward, as if he had ever hesitated in the first place. In April, he entered Fort Marks, stripped down the Spanish flag and raised the Stars and Stripes. Then he pushed on through marsh and swamp, pursuing the Indians, pursuing the Spaniards, and entered Pensacola in triumph on the 28th of May.

It was not fair, he said, to punish the "poor ignorant savages," and not the men who incited them. He arrested and clamped into irons an officer of the Georgia militia who had led the burning of friendly Indian villages. He arrested as "unprincipled villains" a pair of British subjects, whom he accused of arousing the Indians and acting as spies for the Spaniards. Arbuthnot, a peaceful Scottish trader who had warned a personal friend, the Indian Chief Billy Bowlegs, was hanged from the yardarm of his ship. Armbrister, an Englishman who had actually led the Indians into battle, was charged with making "war against the United States," blindfolded with his own necktie, and shot.

This was hardly the end of the affair. Explosions resounded over the cabinets of three countries: England, Spain, and the United States. Embarrassed England finally brushed the whole matter off; but Spain declared that Jackson had attacked "in the most revolting manner." And Calhoun, angry and aware of how close the incident might have brought the country to war, demanded an inquiry, although he had seen Jackson's original letter. The wayward General was defended by Secretary of State John Quincy

Adams with such vigor and eloquence that he convinced the American people and even convinced Spain. Outrages had justified the action. Jackson got off with a mild Presidential reprimand. He had been right to follow the Indians into Florida, but wrong to seize Spanish territory.

The House, however, debated the issue for some twenty-seven days. Leading off was Henry Clay of Kentucky, who denounced "military chieftans," and warned darkly of Caesar, Napoleon, and Oliver Cromwell. All this was campaign oratory, the House knew very well, for Mr. Clay was the political favorite of the West and had no desire whatever to be replaced by Andrew Jackson. In the end, the House voted to uphold the General, but from that day on, Jackson hated no one on earth so much as he hated Henry Clay. Jackson had arrived in Washington by this time, and a Senate inquiry died down when the rumor got around that he would slice off the ears of any Senator who opposed him!

What finally happened was that as the result of a treaty with Spain, East and West Florida were formally annexed to the United States in July 1821. Andrew Jackson was named governor of the new territory. Frankly, Monroe had wanted to get the troublesome hero out of the way, far away, perhaps as ambassador to Russia. He had consulted Thomas Jefferson, who had grimly warned that with Jackson as ambassador we would have a quarrel with Russia in a month. So he was sent to Florida and the United States had a quarrel with Spain in a month.

He journeyed down by way of New Orleans, where a theater rang with "Vive Jackson," and a crown of laurel was placed on his head. Then, for the third time, he entered Pensacola, with its old ruined houses and mixed races and babble of French and Spanish tongues, its beautiful bay and the cooling breeze from the sea. But he was not happy there. Rachel, an ardent Presbyterian, became shocked by the Roman Catholic merrymaking on Sunday. Jackson spoiled the fun by clamping down a set of Blue Laws which closed the theaters and gambling houses, at least on the Sabbath. An argument with the former Spanish Governor ended with that astonished official being dumped in jail for the night. The two had misunderstood each other, Jackson knowing no Spanish and Cavella no English, but to the American public this was only one more example of Andrew Jackson's "energy and promptitude."

Jackson had had enough. In October he resigned his governorship and came home—to the great valley "smiling with fields" and watered by the Cumberland, home to the dark forest-covered mountains, home to the Hermitage, for what he believed to be the last time. He was fifty-four. His stomach was still in an uproar, his cough constant, his lung inflamed. "I do hope they will now leave Mr. Jackson alone," Rachel said. "He is not a well man . . . He has done his share for the country."

He had. He had helped shape a state; he had won a famous victory, and he had made safe for the United States the whole vast domain between Ohio and the Gulf. He had earned the peace that he was enjoying: the leisurely breakfasts, the slow readings of the newspapers, the evenings in his rocking chair, the company of his eleven-year-old adopted son and his nephew, Andrew Jackson "Jack" Donelson, a West Point graduate. The new Hermitage was rising, a stately two-story brick building, with a double gallery supported by tall white columns, but still reflecting "the simple tastes of the farmer." He had built it for Rachel; he did not expect to live to enjoy it.

Someone hinted that Jackson was not "safe" from becoming President. His keen blue eyes blazed up; he ran his hands through his bristling hair. "No, sir . . . I'm not vain enough for that," he said. The thought almost made him angry. "Do they think I am such a damned fool as to think myself fit for President of the United

States?" He could command men in a rough way, but that was all. And Rachel mourned: "They . . . talk everlastingly about [his] being President . . . I can say only, the Lord's will be done."

It had been Aaron Burr, as far back as 1815, who had written, "Jackson's success is inevitable." In 1818, a leading Washington newspaper, *Niles' Register* had taken note of Jackson's "unbounded popularity in the West" and had declared him "a more extraordinary person than has ever appeared in our history." He had "no ambition but for the good of his country." The inevitable was foreshadowed during a wildly triumphant tour of the East in 1819, one "ceaseless ovation" for "the savior of New Orleans," the crowds so great he could scarcely push through the streets, New York showering him with wreaths and trophies.

Ideas now began to occur to the men of Tennessee. Foremost among these was Jackson's friend Major William B. Lewis, who campaigned for seven years to put the General into the White House. He wanted nothing; he asked for nothing. He simply believed that Andrew Jackson was the greatest general and the greatest American who ever lived. So, under the lead of this unofficial campaign manager and would-be President-maker, a group of dedicated Tennesseans decided to go over the heads of the leaders and rouse Jackson "fever" among the American people.

First they approached Jackson. They asked him if there was any unknown reason that would prevent his name from being brought forward? He did not reply. Privately, he said: "My cough sticks by me and the pain in my side and shoulder." But duty was the guiding star of Andrew Jackson. Although he was not a candidate, he said, when the people called, the citizen was bound to render the service demanded.

It was only 1822, and the election was still two long years away. This did not matter. In the aftermath of Monroe's "Era of Good Feeling," there were no issues, only personalities. For there were no parties, only the one National Republican party of Thomas Jefferson, the Federalists having died in disgrace after the Hartford Convention of 1815. What was shaping up was a contest of regions and from each sector of the growing Union the candidates were falling into line.

"Four states sent their nags in . . . Why not Tennessee put in her stud?" demanded the Nashville *Whig*. The candidates were assembling: Henry Clay, the popular "Harry of the West," the blithe, dazzling, eloquent son of a dancing-school teacher, who would help himself from a justice's snuffbox while arguing before the Supreme

Court; New England's John Quincy Adams, who carried his head "like a bull ready to charge"; Secretary of the Treasury William H. Crawford of Georgia, the favorite of "Mr. Jefferson" and the other party leaders; and the young, ardent, and "captivating" John C. Calhoun.

Technically, Jackson was the fifteenth man to toss his hat in the ring, when the Tennessee legislature put forward the name of its favorite son, "the soldier, the statesman, and the honest man." And there was no unanimity for him even in his home state. It was believed that he would carry too much sail in a calm, and this was pretty much the view throughout the country. If the nation were under martial law, the New York *Evening Post* believed, Jackson would be the ideal President. John Quincy Adams thought that the Vice-Presidency would make a more suitable retirement for the General's old age, and certainly there he could "hang no one." Few took his candidacy seriously. It was men long eminent in the ruling circles whom party leaders viewed as Presidential material. "Great General, but unfit for civil employment," was a typical opinion. "President—absurd!" A poll of members of the Electoral College put him far down the line.

But the "westerners" at old Fort Pitt, the river town beyond the mountains, remembered Jackson and his flatboats. The coal miners, small farmers, industrial "mechanics," riverboat men, all stirred with interest at the slogan: "Old Hickory, the Nation's Hero and the People's Friend!" These were "the people," a strange, new, unpredictable element in politics. Certainly, the people had never before really counted in a Presidential election. The party leaders had merely selected from among themselves the candidates to be voted upon and that was it. That was the way Crawford was finally nominated. As for Jackson, did killing Indians and fighting the British thereby make him the "wisest and greatest man in the nation?"

The months wore on, and suddenly the impossible began to happen. The tide swerved in Pennsylvania, where a mass meeting had been called in the town of Carlisle to endorse young John C. Calhoun. Someone moved that Jackson's name be put up instead, and the assembly rose and roared its approval. The movement then spread to Philadelphia and to Harrisburg. In the end, making "a virtue out of necessity," Calhoun dropped out of the race entirely and decided to seek the Vice-Presidency, an office to which he was triumphantly elected.

Yet what had looked like a great mass uprising was so beautifully and skillfully managed, and so secretly that not even the party leaders knew what was going on. This was the first "amateur" campaign for the Presidency. However, to remain in the public eye Jackson had had to return to public life, so in 1823 the Tennessee legislature sent him back to his old seat in the Senate. He arrived in Washington, with the informal polls now showing a Jackson sweep even in Henry Clay's Kentucky, and with posters up, on which were emblazoned, "Old Hickory, last of the Revolutionary patriots." He wrote to Rachel, "My Love," telling her of the great crowds halting his stage, and promised never to separate from her again "in this world." Immediately upon his arrival, he became the "most conspicuous personage in Washington."

The climax came at a brilliant party given in January 1824 by the long-harassed Secretary of State to honor the hero of New Orleans. Jackson was the "star of the evening," and about that time the idea became rooted in the public mind that here was a possible President of the United States. Obviously, the thought had never seriously crossed the mind of Mr. John Quincy Adams. But the Adamses had always been more notable for their statecraft than for their political sagacity.

This was a changed Jackson, grave, reserved;

to Daniel Webster of Massachusetts his manners seemed "more presidential than those of any of the candidates." Frontier ways were out now; he made his peace with an old enemy from the War of 1812, General Winfield Scott, who was haunting the corriders hoping for a duel. As an avowed candidate, Jackson went shopping for suitable attire: cashmere pantaloons and silk to cover his coat buttons. The next season, true to his promise, Rachel joined him. They renewed acquaintance with Lafayette, who visited the capital in 1824. Of him, "Aunt Rachel" reported he "wears a little wig . . . eats hearty, goes to every party . . . every night." Between fifty and one hundred people called on the Jacksons daily, but they only went out to church. A rumor about Mrs. Jackson was silenced by the General in the old way: "I know how to defend her."

Election Day, then as now, was in November. But there was no certain news on election night, or the next week, or even by the next month. The votes came slowly from afar, brought in by flatboat, by post riders, by stage, in saddlebags, slowly, so slowly. The result was not yet clear when Senator Jackson arrived in Washington, on December 7th, after his summer vacation at the Hermitage. He had himself been quietly sure that he would win, but there was no such certainty in the rest of the country. Then the votes mounted; a pattern began to shape itself. Jackson had won. That is, he had won more electors, more states, and more votes than any other candidate, but not a clearcut majority. The election would have to go into the House of Representatives, and Jackson's old enemy Henry Clay ruled the House. Not the people, but Henry Clay would choose the next President of the United States.

Now began the bargaining and the dealing and the double-dealing. A friend of Henry Clay's approached Jackson to talk of an alliance. Rather than become President that way, the General roared, he would "see the earth open and swallow Mr. Clay" and himself. Someone suggested something scandalous about Mrs. Adams. "I never war on females," said Jackson, "and it is only the base and cowardly that do."

Ten days before the vote was to be counted, Henry Clay made his choice, according to the ways and rules by which Presidents had been chosen before. There was genuine fear of Jackson's violent temper and lack of schooling; the Harvard-educated Adams was, without doubt, the better qualified man. But a wild storm of indignation arose from the people, and when Clay announced the decision in favor of Adams in the domed House Chamber, hisses broke out and the galleries had to be cleared.

Adams received his notification, shaking, with the sweat rolling down his face. Jackson remained calm. He could understand Clay's desire to put down a rival and he had a genuine respect for Adams as "a virtuous, able and honest man." At a White House party that night Adams was there, but everyone was looking at Jackson, who greeted the victor in perfect good humor. Adams was distant and cool.

Then, a few days later, came the news that President Adams had chosen Henry Clay for his Secretary of State. Jackson raged. The "Judas of the West" had taken his thirty pieces of silver after all; and from that time on, Jackson and a large majority of the country believed that a corrupt bargain had been made. Clay had sold the Presidency to Adams in return for the State Department. "I could not doubt the facts," Jackson said. He had his issue now for the next campaign, and in 1824, the election contest of 1828 was already underway.

Jackson returned to the Hermitage, an aging man with an invalid wife. Once the Hermitage had meant rest, refuge; now it was only winter quarters. But visitors were still enjoying his gracious hospitality. To the Hermitage, one day, came an old man who looked with dim eyes on a pair of pistols that he had once presented to George Washington. "They are in worthy hands," Lafayette said at last.

Jackson clasped the pistols and Lafayette's hand to his chest. "Yes, I believe myself worthy of them," he said, "if not for what I have done, at least for what I wished to do for my country."

Meanwhile, the surge to Jackson's banner was like a flood. The top party leader in New York, Martin Van Buren, had swung over and other leaders were coming in, from New Hampshire to Georgia. All the "outs" were for Jackson anyway, and now central committees sprang up in every state. Pro-Jackson newspapers were started, and established papers were won over. The corrupt bargain story was revived and repeated at fish frys, barbecues, militia musters. In the off-year election of 1826 Jackson men made heavy gains, but Jackson meanwhile followed advice to "say nothing and plant cotton."

It was all too much for the Adams forces. They struck back—and for two years the mudslinging went on. The big business interests, most of the press, the aristocracy, the wealth, the learning of the country all were against Jackson—everything but the people. Jackson had charged bribery and corruption; this was dirty politics, and they could play dirty politics too. They charged Jackson with being an illiterate, a maniac, an atheist, and a slave trader. The gory ghosts of Dickinson and Woods, Arbuthnot and Ambrister and the six militiamen walked again. It was charged that Jackson had spent "the prime of his life in gambling, in cock-fighting, in horse-racing," and worst of all, that he had torn "from a husband the wife of his bosom." For this last, Jackson believed Adams and Clay to be personally responsible, and he never forgave either of them. Rachel's peace and happiness were shattered forever.

The Jackson people formed committees to meet the charges. They published the full facts of Rachel's tragic life with Robards, her flight, the supposed divorce and marriage, all truthfully and frankly. Meanwhile, at home there was more trouble; young Andrew, Jr., was running up huge debts; a nephew, Andrew Jackson Hutchings, was expelled from college; and the Indian ward, Lincoyer had died. But the political news was beginning to come in and it was inevitable and overwhelming. There was but one issue in the election of 1828—Andrew Jackson. This time the people made a clearcut choice, and John Quincy Adams was returned to private life. Jackson's majority was so great that the result was clear by the

10th of November. Some states divided their ballots, but the overall total in electoral votes was Adams, 83; Jackson, 178. Andrew Jackson would be the next President of the United States. Fat, weary, sick, Rachel said: "For Mr. Jackson's sake, I am glad." But the fates were not yet done with Rachel.

The ladies of Nashville swooped down on her to make her an inaugural gown. The ladies of Cincinnati sent her a lace veil. There was talk of a Presidential coach and six white horses. Then somehow, some way, she seems to have found and read one of the filthy pamphlets her husband had hidden from her. Friends found her hysterical, "crouching in a corner." She bathed her eyes so Jackson would not know. On December 17th she suffered a heart attack, and the agony went on for sixty terrible hours with pain and more pain. Jackson scarcely left her side.

On the 22nd, she rallied somewhat and sat up and smoked with Jackson. Nashville was in gala array for a big victory dinner that was to be given to him. He must get some sleep, Rachel said. Five minutes after he had left the room Rachel screamed. Her head fell upon her maid's shoulder. It was as if Jackson's own heart had burst. He rushed back to her side and lifted her to the bed. A doctor bent over and looked up helplessly.

By midnight friends and relatives began to arrive. They found Jackson "grieving," his head in his hands. His eyes were dry. Now and then his shaking hand would reach out and touch Rachel's cold forehead. Now, at last, he knew the terrible price he had paid for his victory. "Nothing mattered. Nothing would ever matter any more."

It was the greatest funeral in the history of Tennessee, and the tribute was not for Jackson alone. Thousands choked the roads on foot and in buggies to pay their last respects to the beloved "Aunt Rachel." In Nashville, the flags sank to halfmast. And in the yard of the little brick Presbyterian church near the Hermitage, Jackson stood taut, dimly hearing the preacher speak of Rachel's "tender and feeling heart . . . She could have received no pleasure in giving pain to her detractors."

As Rachel was laid to rest in the garden of the Hermitage, now at last the tears began to run down Jackson's worn face. "These tears are due her," he said. "She has shed many for me." Once before, in those bitter months, he had wept, when the filth of the campaign had even slandered the good name of his mother.

"My heart is nearly broke," he admitted. As he started the long journey to Washington, Rachel's miniature was on a black cord around his neck, around his sleeve the black band that he would wear always. He had "aged twenty years in a night." All he could remember now was his sweet young love, to be enshrined forever in his memory. Nearly forty years they had lived together, and for all their strains and sorrows, not a harsh word had passed between them. Now all was over, and it was his own pride, his own yen for glory, he believed, that had helped kill her. But his was not the primary guilt. "May Almighty God forgive her murderers," he burst out. "I never can." He turned his face to the east and set out for Washington.

8

Jacksonian Democracy

IN THAT WINTER of 1828–29, official Washington trembled and waited for the arrival of Andrew Jackson, the most loved and the most hated, the most admired and most feared man in the United States. America had chosen a President straight out of the backwoods; the day of revolution, the people knew, was at hand. Daniel Webster put the popular fears into words:

> General Jackson will be here abt. 15. of Feb.
> Nobody knows what he will do.
> My opinion is
> That when he comes he will bring a breeze with him.
> Which way it will blow I cannot tell.

Rumors of the General's "advance" filled the city. A British writer saw him in Cincinnati, his hair blowing, and looking "like a gentleman and a scholar." But many travelers were horrified at the "brutul familiarity" to which he was subjected and the mobs fighting to tug at his hand.

A "big entry" was planned for February 12th. This was forestalled by Jackson's friend, Senator John Henry Eaton of Tennessee, who secretly sent his carriage to Maryland for the General, and got the frail hero safely installed at Gadsby's Tavern in Washington before the cannon could begin to boom. A wild feeling was sweeping Jackson's admirers, as if the country was about to be saved "from some dreadful danger." Barbers advertised haircuts "in the Jackson style." One thing was sure—the Era of Good Feeling was over. Jackson had even refused to pay the customary call on the retiring President, so Mr. Adams did not attend the Inauguration and left the city unnoticed and alone.

Inauguration Day dawned bright and clear, but with snow enough left to make mud on the ground. Looking out of the Tavern window, Jackson could see the length of Pennsylvania Avenue he must march. At one end was the Capitol, and at the four corners of the White House, the brick buildings of the State, Treasury, War, and Navy Departments. Between them were a scatter of houses and the muddy stretch of the Avenue, now black with people. Many were singing what was to become one of the first campaign songs,

"We're walking down to Washington/To shake hands with President Jackson." To Jackson, they looked familiar enough in their boots and homespun and coon-skin caps, the faces of Irish immigrants and Northwest fur traders, mountain men and hunters and old soldiers, but all as terrifying to official Washington as the invasion of Vandals and Goths had been to the ancient Romans. Jackson himself might have experienced a grim moment of enjoyment as he thought of Chief Justice John Marshall who would administer the Presidential oath. For Marshall, spokesman for power and privilege, had said: "The wild asses from the West, led by Andy Jackson, will ruin the government."

Now at last the cannon could boom. And as Jackson moved along the Avenue, tall, stooped, his white hair blowing, the true greatness of the man silenced even the scoffers. On the Capitol steps he bowed to the people with a grace and dignity "which I never saw surpassed," an amazed South Carolinian declared. He lifted the Bible and kissed it, as the grimly disapproving Chief Justice swore him in, but few could hear the words of his inaugural address, although they could see the papers tremble as he turned them. Finally, he mounted a horse and rode down the Avenue, with a yipping mob at his heels.

A mural in the U.S. Capitol depicts Jackson's swearing in as president on March 4, 1829. Chief Justice John Marshall administers the oath of office.

Cakes and ice cream and orange punch were being served in the East Room of the White House for the ladies and gentlemen who were expected to attend. Instead, it was the people off the streets who broke through the lines of guards and burst in, ripping clothes, smashing china and glasses, and muddying $150 chairs with their boots as they climbed up on the seats to get a look at their President. Women fainted. Finally, someone noticed Jackson, "sinking into a listless state of exhaustion." Men linked arms and took him out through the rear. But the only way to get the people out was to move the tubs of punch onto the lawn. Finally, a more sedate inaugural ball closed the festivities.

This near riot at the White House was the first shock. The next came with the announcement of the Presidential Cabinet—a cabinet chosen exactly as those in the past had been chosen, and thus entirely different. Earlier Cabinets had been composed of the statesmen who elected the President. This one, too, was made up of the men who had elected the President. Party henchmen most of them, only the names of Vice-President Calhoun and the new Secretary of State, New York's former Senator Martin Van Buren, were familiar to the public.

Not that Jackson had not chosen some good men. There was, for instance, in what turned out to be the appropriate post of Secretary of War, young Senator John Henry Eaton of Tennessee. An unusually able man and graduate of the University of North Carolina at Chapel Hill, Eaton was even possessed of some literary talent: he was Jackson's official biographer. But Mr. Eaton had a personal problem, which would soon turn out to be a national problem as well. He had, therefore, approached Jackson for advice, wondering if he should even accept the post in the Cabinet. But Jackson reassured him: there would be no difficulties whatever.

The country, meanwhile, was somewhat reassured with the announcement of the President's program, he having run on no platform at all. He pledged to collect a long overdue debt from France; to push the Indians westward (always a popular idea), to seek a compromise on the ever-troublesome question of the tariff, and to pay off the national debt. But there was an ominous question mark in his demand for some new kind of agency to replace the United States Bank, a privately operated institution which had the use of the federal funds. Why this? Jackson had a reputation in the West as a sound money man. The Bank's charter still had six years to run, and the Bank president, Nicolas Biddle, had supported Andrew Jackson.

The people wondered, but there was a lot to wonder about with Jackson in the White House. What counted, as it turned out, was his almost uncanny ability to make his causes the causes of the people as a whole; and a Supreme Court Justice marveled at the "paralyzing swiftness with which the translates thoughts into action." He was the dominant figure in official Washington, "tall, slim, straight," his face deeply lined, his mouth taut, his hair standing erect, as if stiffened "with his defiant spirit." Despite his grief and boneweariness, he gave an overwhelming impression of "energy and daring."

He was still the dominant figure in a city used to striking personalities: in the Washington of Henry Clay, with his ever-present snuff box and his indescribable charm; of "Black Dan" Webster, his brow "the very dome of thought"; of Calhoun, "erect, slim, stern and resolute"; of the polished and engaging Robert Young Hayne and the pompous and pugnacious Thomas Hart Benton with his tremendous backlog of courage and vitality. Since Jackson's recent term as Senator their old quarrel had been patched up; now Benton was to become the foremost supporter of the Administration in Congress and a loyal friend to Jackson as well.

And this was also the Washington of Mr. Martin Van Buren. Mr. Van Buren had been advised not to enter the Jackson Administration. He was warned that it was foredoomed to failure. Mr. Van Buren liked to win. Mr. Van Buren was always good-natured, always smiling, always hoping there would be no bad feelings. He was a political boss out of New York, a state that had produced some good ones, the Clintons, for instance, and

Aaron Burr. And he was a compromiser like Henry Clay, who enjoyed nothing so much as bringing together the most diehard opponents. Van Buren knew the art of politics to perfection and was sure that he could bend and control the political amateur in the White House.

As a Senator, Van Buren had served in Congress with Jackson, but the General's close cronies had been southern and western men. Now as his Secretary of State, it was time for Van Buren to be on closer terms with his former colleague. Soon after Inauguration Day, he came to call at the White House.

He found the new President looking old, tired, and careworn. And indeed Jackson had much to brood over. Although Jack and Emily Donelson's children filled the house, and little feet raced up and down the stairs, Jackson was sad. He had had to reprimand his young niece and pretty White House hostess, Emily. Andrew Jackson Hutchings had been expelled from still another school. Big Sam Houston, whom he had loved like a son, had resigned the governorship of Tennessee after the collapse of an unfortunate marriage, and in disgrace had vanished into the wilderness. Tennessee . . . the Hermitage . . . Did the willows grow on Rachel's grave?

Van Buren once again was struck by the courtliness of this "noble old man," weariness dropped away in a flash, and whose only insistance was that they must do no business tonight. Mr. Van Buren had just arrived from New York and must not overtire himself. Van Buren saw right away that the tragedy of Rachel's death had molded Jackson into a man who not only feared nothing and hoped for nothing, but to whom even pain meant nothing any more. He could be cajoled, perhaps, and won; but, above all he needed a friend who would help. Mr. Van Buren decided to be that friend.

Although no athlete, Van Buren showed his genius by going out immediately and buying a saddle horse, so he could accompany the President on his rides. Then he offered a suggestion. The diplomatic corps had been terrified by the election of a frontier President and a military chieftain in the tradition of Napoleon. Why not give them a private reception. The Executive did and they succumbed to his charm, even as Van Buren had done, and found Jackson's remarks so pleasing that they even requested copies to take home. A final touch was when Jackson decided to keep John Quincy Adams' French cook!

But there were many who were less pleased.

"Spoils" and removals were the order of the day. In the past, men who had helped elect a president went to the Cabinet or the Supreme Court or on foreign missions; why should not this same principle be applied to the "vast horde" of "very small fry" who had elected Jackson? Even Thomas Jefferson had noted that officeholders seldom resigned; and the basic, underlying principle of Jacksonian democracy was that one man was as fit as another to hold public office.

So the big job of distribution of the spoils got underway. Jackson had some very good reasons, aside from politics, for some of his removals. In an "Outline of Principles," sent to every department head, he had ordered that all possible "economies and improvements" be made and surplus offices dropped. In any event, the dust had to be swept out of the corners. For example, the Register of the Treasury had been in federal employ since the American Revolution, yet had stolen some $10,000. Under those conditions, Jackson said, "I would turn out my own father."

The first auditor was seldom seen sober. Several employees of the Treasury had taken money; some office-holders had gone bankrupt twelve times in a few months, and eighty-seven had been to jail. Jackson sharply reprimanded a clergyman who sought a job; if he attended to his own work, the President reminded him, he would have no time for anything else.

Van Buren had been thought to be against the removals, because he had sent a pack of office-seekers home. But the removals went rapidly on, and the soft-footed Mr. Van Buren was behind many of them. Some injustices were done. Many small officeholders never knew of their removal until they found new men holding their jobs. As for Van Buren, before the year was out, Jackson was writing that he was "everything that I could desire him to be . . . frank, open, candid, and manly." One day when they were riding together, Jackson's horse stumbled and "Matty" saved his President from a bad fall. Grimly, Jackson observed that maybe saving such a life as his was no favor. He had won all the honors his country could give him, and yet he had no desire to live.

He had troubles enough certainly to make him miserable. Yet one thing at least that looked like tragedy to him was actually the musical comedy of the Jackson Administration. The problem concerned John Eaton, the Secretary of War, or, to be more exact, his "strikingly beautiful" and witty young bride.

Since her fourteenth year, when Dolly Madison had called her "the prettiest girl in Washington," Peggy O'Neale, a tavern keeper's daughter, had been the talk, if not the toast, of the town. A nephew of a Cabinet officer had killed himself over the plump, rosy-cheeked brunette with the beautifully expressive blue eyes. Two Army officers had almost fought a duel over her, and an elderly general suffered a broken heart. In succession, she had almost eloped with a major and a captain, but at sixteen was safely married to a "tall blond Adonis" named John Timberlake. She had known him almost a month! Still in her teens, she was rumored to have had romances enough for a dozen women, and the shocked Mrs. James Monroe told her she was unwelcome at the White House.

A longtime family friend, and for ten years a lodger at Major O'Neale's Franklin Inn, was the young Congressman from Tennessee, John Henry Eaton. He had helped Peggy's father out of financial difficulties when he had almost lost the tavern; and after Timberlake had cost his father-in-law some $15,000, the obliging family friend got him off to sea as a Naval purser. After a wild spree in a port in the Mediterranean, Timberlake cut his own throat, in protest, it was rumored, over his wife's friendship with Senator Eaton.

"Anxious and distressed," Eaton had approached Jackson; how could he calm down the ugly talk? Jackson was furious: Peggy had been a pet of his and Rachel's when they had stayed at her father's inn, and after Rachel's sufferings, nothing could rouse Jackson more than malicious slander of a woman. He had advised Eaton: "If you love Margaret Timberlake . . . marry her forthwith . . . and shut their mouths." In January 1829, the couple was married, and, so far as official Washington was concerned, it had just begun.

For Peggy was now a "Cabinet lady." The Cabinet led society, and Peggy had never been admitted into society. The snubbing began at the inaugural ball. Then the Cabinet ladies would not call on Peggy, nor would they receive her when she called. Jackson got angrier and angrier. He instructed his Cabinet officers to order their wives to call upon Peggy. He even visited the Vice-President's wife and laid down the law. Imperious little Floride Calhoun merely showed him the door. He even demanded the recall of a foreign minister who would not sit at Peggy's side.

He had urged the marriage; now he tried to force open the doors of official society. In earlier days, Eaton had defended Jackson's beloved Rachel; Eaton was the last person on earth he would desert. When a clergyman wrote the President, hinting of Peggy's bad reputation, Jackson read the gentleman of the cloth a furious lecture on Christian charity and got out of his church. "All the pain, all the helpless, pent-up fury" of his tragic days with Rachel burst forth, and once more his tongue became a stinging lash. His championship of "Bellona, The Goddess of War," drained the energy he needed for more important things. So angry at the Cabinet officers that he almost never called them into session, because their wives were snubbing Peggy, Jackson was doing virtually all the official business himself. He acted as his own Secretary of War, replacing the musket with the far more accurate rifle as the Army's standard weapon. He was his own Secretary of State, dealing personally with Britain and France, and his own Secretary of the Treasury.

Just what Peggy was guilty of was never quite clear, except of being young, pretty, and of using the President's friendship to advance her social designs. Jackson's niece and White House hostess, Mrs. Jack Donelson, was disgusted by Peggy's boldness and talk of affection for the President. Finally she, too, declined to receive her. "Go back to Tennessee, my dear," the President said, and the whole Donelson family departed. Racked by headaches, unable to sleep, Jackson paced about the silent and gloomy White House, looking where "the cradle of my little pet" had been and her "little waggon." At night he would sit holding family letters, or looking at the babies' pictures. Heartsick over the loss, of both Jack Donelson, his secretary and favorite nephew, and the "sweet little ones," Jackson humbled his pride and begged the family to return. All the uproar over Peggy, he said, had become a political plot to destroy him.

This was true. Even Mrs. John C. Calhoun had been quite willing to call upon Mrs. Eaton until the political implications of the turmoil revealed themselves. All those who supported Jackson lined up for Peggy; those against him were against her. Meanwhile, the functioning of the government had slowed almost to a standstill.

It was Mr. Van Buren who offered a solution. Mr. Van Buren was no slanderer of women. A widower, he had wined Peggy and dined her. Giving her the place of honor at his dinner table, he had forever sealed his place in Jackson's heart. Now, on a long horseback ride, he outlined his plan. He would resign as Secretary of State. He was sure the others would be quick to resign and the problem of official society would be solved. Jackson protested; he did not want to lose Van Buren, but the "Little Magician" insisted. And his magic worked. He gave a supper for the loyal Cabinet members, supposedly to consult with them and announced his plan. Suddenly, Eaton said: "Gentlemen, this is all wrong. I am the one who ought to resign." He did; eventually, they all did. Eaton and Peggy were sent to the Court of Spain and Van Buren was appointed minister to England.

But the bitterness in the wake of the affair died hard. Vice-President John C. Calhoun, who had lost his chief's friendship, took this occasion to strike back, and to cast a deciding vote against Senate confirmation of the appointment of the controversial Van Buren. "It will kill him, sir, kill him dead," Calhoun said gleefully. The shrewd Thomas Hart Benton countered: "You have broken a Minister, and elected a Vice-President." And he had. Public sympathy rallied to the embarrassed Van Buren, already at his post in England and forced to come home as a sacrifice to political bitterness. But Jackson took his own course of action; for the upcoming election of 1832, he dropped Calhoun from the ticket and chose Martin Van Buren as his running mate.

One upshot of the Eaton affair was that an excellent new Cabinet was appointed, including Edward Livingston as Secretary of State and Roger Taney as Attorney-General. But in the long months of distrust of his "official family," Jackson had come to rely more and more upon his "kitchen cabinet," a group of strictly honest, hardworking, devotedly loyal, and magnificently skillful politicians. All of them not only admired Jackson but actually loved him, for his gift for making friends was as great as his ability to make enemies. Singly or as a group they could best most of the leading political figures of the day. They included the white-haired, half-crippled Amos Kendall, editor of *Western America*, the little one-hundred-pound Francis Blair of the Washington *Globe,* a Yankee newspaperman named Isaac Hill, and such assorted figures as Eaton, Van Buren, Benton, and a young Congressman from Tennessee named James Knox Polk.

9

The Union Preserved

JACKSON HAD NEED of all the help his "brain trust" could give him, for the great questions of his Administration were beginning to arise. First of all, the civilized Indians of the East were becoming as big a problem as the uncivilized ones of the West. The Cherokees, Creeks, and Seminoles that Jackson had broken in war had become a challenge in peace. They were *too* civilized and hence posed a competitive threat to the settlers. They lived in Georgia, Alabama, and Mississippi on rich lands the white man envied. Borders had never been respected on the frontier. Now it was the whites who were attacking, burning, killing, and tearing up treaties. The "savages" fought—through the courts. They fought and they won in the United States Supreme Court, at which point Jackson is supposed to have said: "John Marshall has made his decision; now let him enforce it."

The fact is, the President was supposed to have enforced the decision, but he did not even try to do so. "Your great white father cannot, nor can Congress," Jackson told the chiefs. He made them generous offers of money and territory if they would, of their own free will, move to a land "of promise and peace" beyond the Mississippi. In the end, most of them did so, many dying tragically on their way along the so-called "Trail of Tears." Jackson knew perfectly well that the white man would no longer let the Indian live beside him. But in giving way to the states, he had given encouragement to a doctrine that all but wrecked Jacksonian democracy.

The doctrine was nullification, or, as it is often called, interposition—the right of a state to decide whether or not a federal law was legal and whether or not to obey. Thomas Jefferson had invented the doctrine. South Carolina brought it forward in 1828 in a curious document called "The South Carolina Exposition and Protest," written to oppose the federal tariff law. Tariffs, or taxes on foreign goods brought into the country, had long been demanded by the new and struggling American industries in the Northeast, and the tariffs were getting higher all the time. The trouble was that the South sold its cotton and tobacco at low prices set by the markets of the world and preferred to buy low-cost tools, furniture, and clothes from Europe, rather than pay high prices for American-made products. But with a high tariff on them, foreign goods turned out to be just as expensive. Now South Carolina was making a test case, and the big question was—what would Andrew Jackson do? He was a Southerner. He had promised to lower the tariff, and he was known to be a dear friend of the young South Carolina champion of the nullification idea, Senator Robert Hayne.

On a wintery day in January 1830, Major Lewis wandered into the White House. "How is Webster getting on?" asked Jackson.

"Demolishing our friend Hayne," was the prompt answer.

"I expected it," the President retorted.

Daniel Webster of Massachusetts had only accidentally heard the words of Hayne's speech. Lounging against a pillar after a morning of profitable law practice before the Supreme Court, the New Englander suddenly heard something that interested him and sat down. Hayne, tall, blond, buoyant, was making his speech a charming thing of grace and satire, but his support of the idea of nullification was unmistakably clear. Webster listened intently, then the next day gave a brief retort to Hayne, who followed up with a major speech afterwards. He reminded Webster of his own youthful days, when the New Englander had voiced the right of his section to oppose the War of 1812. Hayne cited precedent and history to "prove" the nullification idea. Calhoun, who had secretly written the original South Carolina "Protest," sent Hayne notes and smiled down on him from the Vice-Presidential chair. Daniel Webster did not smile.

A great crowd filled the Senate Chamber the day that Webster, a dramatic figure in his blue coat with brass buttons, his great dark eyes glowing, arose to make his "reply to Hayne." He lacked Hayne's warmth, but the majesty of his manner, his Milton-like phrases, and his keen logic resulted in one of "the world's masterpieces of formal oratory." Nullification, he declared flatly, was unconstitutional, impractical, and ruinous to the idea of the Union. When his eyes last looked on the heavens, he said, he did not want to see the "states dissevered, discordant, belligerent . . . a land . . . drenched . . . in fraternal blood," but rather, the flag of his country, "not a stripe erased . . . not a star obscured." Jackson said nothing, but Webster's words thrilled the old hero in the White House no less than they stirred the country.

Jackson's own chance for an answer to nullification came at the annual Jefferson Day dinner two months later in April. He was waiting for it; the Nullifiers were waiting for him. Many of Jackson's friends: Hayne, the newspaperman, Duff Green, even Benton, were more or less sympathetic to the states' rights idea. Officially, Jackson had, as yet, said nothing, but privately he recognized nullification as the old question of mutiny all over again. He marched off to the Jefferson Day dinner with the look of a general commanding his troops. The twenty-four formal toasts had been printed up and were so violently nullifications that many of the expected guests came, took one look, and walked away.

But not Jackson. Vice-President Calhoun escorted the President to his seat, and still the President said nothing. He looked pleasant and undisturbed. Calhoun then arose to speak. He delivered a beautiful tribute to Jefferson and heralded Jackson as the living standardbearer of the principles of the Sage of Monticello. Then the toasts began, all twenty-four of them, each building up further the case for states' rights. Jackson sat in silence, his mouth taut. So the Nullifiers thought they could capture the party machinery, did they? And then him? And then the whole country? Did they expect him to sit by? Did they expect that Andrew Jackson would see destroyed the Union for which he had fought and bled and almost died? He heard his name spoken and rose to his feet to make his toast. He was ready for them. He knew what he was going to say. He faced Calhoun; the blue eyes blazed into the brown. "Our Union," Jackson said. "It must and shall be preserved."

He had uttered a declaration of war. He could not wipe out nullification in one sentence, but he could defy it. Within a few moments, two thirds of the diners had fled the room. The battle lines were drawn. And Calhoun's counter-toast came as an anticlimax. "The Union," he said, "next to our liberties, most dear."

The Jefferson Day dinner marked Jackson's final break with Calhoun. It had begun when Calhoun's wife had led the "moral party" fighting Peggy O'Neale Eaton. It had continued when Jackson got hold of an old letter revealing that Calhoun had not been his supporter during his invasion of Florida, but had wanted an official investigation. "My hair stood on end for an hour," Jackson said, after his discovery. And he wrote Calhoun: "Understanding you now, no further communication with you on this subject is necessary."

Calhoun, too, understood. He knew now that he had no hope of any further advancement under the Jackson Administration. There was no need now to conceal his authorship of the "Exposition and Protest," his endorsement of nullification.

Calhoun loved the Union, no less than Jackson did; but he knew South Carolina and the wild hot temper of the state. Lacking an outlet in nullification, South Carolina might well plunge headlong into secession and civil war. Calhoun knew this; Jackson did not. Jackson simply saw nullification as the end of the Union. Against Calhoun's finespun logic, he pitted his own magnificent simplicity; and the people were aware of this—except the people of South Carolina.

Jackson's hand was strengthened for the coming fray by the outcome of the election of 1832. Against the simmering background of the hour, the election itself was almost an anticlimax—interesting because it marked the return of the party system to American politics. True, Henry Clay's supporters still called themselves National Republicans, clinging to the name—and fame—of Jefferson's old party, as Jackson did with his Democratic Republicans. But the divisions—and the parties—were real; there was even a small "third" group, the Anti-Masonic party, in the field. Oddly enough, by the next election the name *Republican* was dropped entirely and the Whigs and the Democrats emerged.

Jackson's victory was more triumphant than his most wildly enthusiastic supporters could have dreamed. He carried sixteen states for 219 electoral votes, as against six states and 88 votes for Henry Clay.

What had happened? In the first place, Clay was a patriot and had no desire to agitate the nullification issue. But he had made his big mistake in thinking that the United States Bank, and Jackson's opposition to it, was the big issue. It *was*, later on. In fact, the Bank people were so bitter that a Washington newspaper actually carried a story that the only way to save the Bank and the nation was to assassinate the President, and it was said that the man who would render this little service to his country would receive a fee of $50,000 from the Bank. Jackson read this, believed it, and grimly checked it away for future reference.

Right now, however, the issue was two-edged: nullification and Jackson. Jackson's Democrats had no platform; *he* was the platform, and the election itself was the least of his worries. "It will be a walk," he said. But there was another victor in the election of 1832—the lame-duck Vice-

President John C. Calhoun. He had resigned from the Vice-Presidency and had himself elected Senator from South Carolina that he might fight Jackson and uphold his doctrine in person.

Calhoun had mapped the way. Back in February 1832, a South Carolina convention had called upon the sons of the rebellious state "to defend her in whatever form she may proclaim her purpose to Resist." This had been the beginning. The actual form the resistance took was the famed Ordinance of November 24, 1832. Very simply, it declared the tariff law null and void. It forbade the state to appeal to the Supreme Court, and announced that customs duties would no longer be paid. Furthermore, if Washington tried to enforce the law, South Carolina would "organize a separate government." Force would be met by force.

To Calhoun, all this was peaceful, legal, and constitutional. To Jackson, it was still mutiny, the climax to the storm that had been blowing up ever since Calhoun had written his "Exposition and Protest." He was all the more convinced when efforts were made in Charleston to lure away loyal Naval forces, and reports came that the Army officers were planning to surrender the harbor forts. Promptly, Jackson, in his capacity as Commander-in-Chief, removed all malcontents, replaced them, and sent Commander of the Army General Winfield Scott (his old enemy) to mobilize for a surprise attack. Seven cutters and a ship of war trained their guns on Charleston's famous Battery, and arms were slipped in for the loyal men in the city. Yet Jackson also moved to ease the causes of the dissension. He signed a bill to gradually lower tariffs and his annual Message was a calm attempt to cool off the hot-heads.

No matter . . . the Nullifiers swept the elections in South Carolina and offers of military service poured into the state capital. The once-loyal Hayne was organizing Mounted Minute Men, while Jackson grimly reflected that the South Carolinians were free to talk and agitate to their heart's content. "But," he promised, "if one drop of blood be shed there in defiance of the laws of the United States I will hang the first man of them I can get my hands on to the first tree I can find."

Still he could not move, for no overt act had, as yet, been committed. He pondered a warning from Van Buren: "You will say I am on my old track—caution—caution—caution: but . . . considering our respective temperaments," Van Buren continued, this advice was the best way he could render service. So Jackson held his fire, although he did mutter to a friend that if this sort of thing went on, the country would be "like a bag of meal with both ends open."

What he could do was talk. He decided to counter South Carolina's Ordinance with a proclamation, addressed to the "fellow-citizens of my native state," as he considered South Carolina to be. Actually it was intended as much for the other Southern states like Virginia, where nullification had taken deep root. He set the most talented man in his Administration, Edward Livingston, to work writing it; the words and the polish were Livingston's, but Jackson infused it with his own fire. As Livingston wrote, Jackson looked over his shoulder. "The Union must be preserved," the President said, "without blood if this be possible, but it must be preserved . . . at any price."

The words of the proclamation thrilled the country. The Constitution formed "a government, not a league," Jackson said. If one state could secede, "the United States is not a nation." Speaking like a father to his children, Jackson warned the Carolinians, "You are deluded by men who are either deceived themselves or wish to deceive you." South Carolina's blood had "cemented this happy union." Would South Carolinians dare give up the protection of their flag, the very name of Americans? The real objective of nullification, according to Jackson, was disunion, and "Disunion by armed force is treason."

Bells rang out; bonfires blazed up. For the moment, even the wealth and respectability of the country was behind Andrew Jackson. Daniel Webster and even bitter old John Quincy Adams praised him. In far-off New Salem, Illinois, a lank young man who looked "as if he was hewn out with an ax," read the proclamation and brooded over it. Abraham Lincoln would remember it when composing his First Inaugural Address.

Now, as it would twenty-nine years later, the nation hovered on the brink of civil war. John C. Calhoun, the symbol of the Southern protest, left his home at Fort Hill to attend the session of Congress that opened in January 1833. Crowds watched him silently as he made his slow journey northward from South Carolina to defend his embattled state. Many thought that he was sentencing himself to death. Jackson, it was said, would seize and imprison him upon his arrival in Washington. Senator Thomas Hart Benton warned a congressman: "When Jackson begins to talk about hanging, [men] can begin to look for ropes."

Pale and taut, but with his voice firm, Calhoun walked into the Senate Chamber on January 4, 1833, and took the oath to protect and defend the Constitution of the United States. Over the next few weeks, in a series of impassioned talks, he convinced the fairminded of his patriotism, if not of the correctness of his cause. If the lean, shaggy-haired South Carolinian deceived his listeners, it was because he himself was deceived. He was certainly no traitor but a fanatic. For he was sure that nullification would preserve the Union, not destroy it, that South Carolina was upholding the Constitution by refusing to obey laws that it thought to be unconstitutional.

He was, he said, against "the dangerous and growing disease" of the strong oppressing the weak; power could only be opposed by power. The question was whether the American system was federal or consolidated, whether the states or the people had made the Constitution and the Union. History, he claimed, showed that the states had, and what powers they had given, they could choose to take away. Nullification was therefore constitutional. It prevented oppression by majorities, as the vote prevented oppression by rulers.

Once again, Daniel Webster rose to the challenge. Again, in majestic, glowing prose, he voiced the cause of the Union. If nullification was invoked, "the whole Union is virtually dissolved." He would tell how the Constitution worked, not what it was intended to be. For all practical purposes, the Constitution had set up a permanent government. "The people of the

United States are one people," Webster said. "They are one in making war and one in making peace." If Mr. Calhoun feared majority rule, did he then want minority rule? Once again, Webster's words stirred the country and warmed the heart of the old soldier in the White House.

Who was right? Calhoun was on the side of the past, of logic and of history, but Webster had spoken for the people and the future and what the people wanted their government to be. Webster would win. However, words alone could not settle the nullification question. Jackson issued a call for action. He sent to the Senate a Force bill, demanding arms to put down rebellion in South Carolina.

Calhoun and the other Southerners met this with bitter defiance. One called Charleston "a beleaguered city." Calhoun, his deep eyes blazing, spoke "under a degree of excitement seldom witnessed," warning that should the "Bloody Bill" be passed, it would be "resisted at every hazard—even that of death!"

It was at this tense moment that Henry Clay, who boasted that he had saved the Union before with his Missouri Compromise in 1820, came up with one of his miracles. He offered a compromise tariff plan. Actually, it was less generous than what Jackson was willing to offer, but it was too late for the embattled Southerners to take concessions from Andrew Jackson. To save face, Calhoun supported Clay's bill; also to save face, Jackson men rammed through the Force bill anyway, and, to save face, all of Calhoun's supporters but one walked out when the vote was called. The compromise tariff was passed. Calhoun, worn to the point of physical collapse, had to board an open mail coach and ride eight days and nights to South Carolina, in the hope that he could get there in time to avert disaster. The day he left, March 3rd, a Victory Ball was held in Charleston for the South Carolina "volunteers," who had pledged to defend the sovereign state against the Union. A nullification convention was assembling in the state capitol at Columbia, ready to pronounce the tariff officially null and void in South Carolina. This, Calhoun knew, would mean the clamping down of the Force bill, invasion, and civil war. If only he could get there in time! He *did* get there in time, and, in the end, he persuaded the South Carolinians to hold off rebellion—for a while.

On March 4th, the temperature in Washington fell to 11 degrees, and in the snow Andrew Jackson went through an inaugural ceremony as quiet as the first had been rowdy. But it was all somehow anticlimactic. That night, reading Rachel's

Bible, the President felt suddenly, terribly weary. Unable to sleep, he made his way to the rooms of the White House babies, the grand-nieces and nephews, his little "pets." Comforted, he looked at them. It was good to know that the Donelsons had come back. It was good to know, too, that the White House was more comfortable for them now, what with the improvements that had been made during the past months: hot and cold running water installed and even shower baths.

Within a few days, a final postscript to nullification was sent him. On March 15, his sixty-sixth birthday, the South Carolina Ordinance was repealed.

Now it was time for him to ride a white horse and be feted as "the saviour of the Union." He endured four days of celebration in Philadelphia, then proceeded eastward. Even in New England, an area less enthusiastic about Jackson and less enthusiastic generally, the cannon boomed in salute. "How old, how very old he looks," was the murmur through the crowds, as they saw his haggard face and white hair. But he had still the look of the outdoor man, and the almost incredible charm of his volcanic personality magnetized even the prejudiced.

A bitter Boston merchant suddenly demanded: "Do someone come and salute the old

In March 1833, Jackson was celebrated as "the savior of the Union." Riding a white horse, the 66-year-old president looked gray and haggard to many in the crowd.

man," and his little granddaughter leaned from the window waving a kerchief. The suspicious president of Harvard University, Josiah Quincy, was charmed completely, describing Jackson as "a knightly personage." But the ever-bitter John Quincy Adams declined to attend and witness the "disgrace," when Harvard conferred an honorary degree upon "a barbarian who could hardly spell his own name," as Mr. Adams put it.

A humorist newspaper writer of the day, "Major Jack" Downing wrote on this unlikely occasion that as the President received the diploma, Jack whispered to him, "You must give 'em a little Latin, *Doctor*!"

Jackson, in Downing's farce, replies, "*E pluribus unum*, my friends, *sine qua non*."

Latin or no Latin, Jackson was so worn out when he reached Salem that Quincy took his place in the presidential carriage during a night parade. The excitement was so great no one seemed to notice. That night, the President collapsed, but although bleeding from the lungs, and weak, he insisted the next day on continuing his tour as far as Concord, New Hampshire. There he gave in at last and started his journey home by steam-boat down the Merrimack. The tour had been a triumph.

10

The Battle of the Bank

MORE WARFARE WAS AWAITING HIM in Washington. Behind the classic Greek columns of a marble temple in Philadelphia was the massed wealth and authority of the most powerful institution in America. This was the Bank of the United States. Though licensed or chartered by the government, the Bank was really a private business corporation. The government had contributed one fifth of the money that originally set it up and could name five of the twenty-five directors. On the other hand, the Bank acted as a treasury or repository for the federal funds, which it could use as it saw fit and upon which it paid no interest. And all this wealth and all this power, to let money out or pull it back in, to make depressions or to cure them, was largely in the hands of one man, the brilliant 47-year-old president of the Bank of the United States, Mr. Nicholas Biddle.

Mr. Biddle was a charmer. He was a suave, sleek, darkly handsome man, who had been a prodigy as a child and a writer and editor in youth. As for banking, his genius was such that he had even been able to wheedle loans for the United States after the burning of Washington in 1812. He loved fine wines and rare old books, beautiful clothes, and the paintings by Gainesborough, West, and Stuart which adorned his walls. "The tastes of an aesthete and the morals of a pirate," it was said of him.

Above all, he loved power. He had ruled the Bank for ten years. He regarded it as *his* bank, the country as his private empire. Backed up by the use of the federal funds, he could keep his own banknotes at high value. He could whip state banks into line, or even close them down by forcing them to make good their paper money with solid coin. He could and did make loans at the right time to the right people, Mr. Webster, for instance, and Mr. Henry Clay.

The West had long been suspicious of Eastern banking power anyway. Jackson was sure now that there were good reasons for the suspicions. What he wanted was "a simple bank of deposit," where the government funds could be kept, with the government in complete control. Such a bank, of course, would be useless as far as business was concerned, for it would have no power to stimulate the economy by giving out money for loans during times of depression or by withholding cash during periods of inflation and boom.

A bill to recharter the Bank had passed the Senate in 1832. Grimly, Jackson worked out a veto message, so exhausting himself that on one occasion when Van Buren came calling, he found him in bed. But the gamecock look was still on the President's face. He took his visitor's hand and ran the other through his bristling hair. "The bank, Mr. Van Buren, is trying to kill me, but I will kill it."

His veto message is one of the great statements in American history defending our democratic philosophy. This was no mere backwoodsman talking, but the President of an entire people. There were and always would be natural differences among men, Jackson said. But when the government itself (and now he claimed that the Bank was a part of the government) made the rich richer and the poor poorer, then the more humble members of society had reason to complain. The Bank had been acting as an instrumentality of the government. And the duty of government was to seek "equal protection and . . . shower its favors alike on the high and the low."

In Congress and across the country the battle

lines massed. The Bank led off, spreading stories of catastrophes to occur if it were not rechartered. Pressure was brought to bear. A meat wholesaler cut his payments to a farmer in half. A Pennsylvania manufacturer laid off his help because of "unsettled conditions," hinting the men would never be rehired until Jackson was put down. Other workers got direct warnings to "vote their bread and butter."

Jackson remained calm. Van Buren noted that fighting the President on this question were the nation's leading orators, the banks, the Supreme Court, the transport system, the manufacturers, the Southern states' righters, and the best-financed political party. Again, nobody was for Jackson but the people.

Jackson feared and detested having so much power concentrated in the hands of a man like Nicholas Biddle. He saw the situation as unconstitutional and "dangerous to liberty." He had become all the more alert during the 1832 presidential campaign. In November of that year, a leading Jackson newspaper, the *New York Courier and Enquirer*, had suddenly switched to Henry Clay and the Bank after a loan of $15,000; and a representative changed his vote in Congress for a similar reason. Quite simply, Jackson was convinced that if the Bank kept on it would use the federal funds to buy up enough votes in Congress to override his veto and put over any program it desired.

In the summer of 1833, Jackson began discussing with his cabinet his plan to remove the government deposits from the Bank. He proposed to start the withdrawals on the first of October. His Secretary of the Treasury, William J. Duane, who was a Biddle man, refused to carry out the President's instructions; and so, on September 23, Jackson replaced him with Roger B. Taney.

"General Jackson's popularity can stand anything," it was always said; but could it? Six months before, farm prices were high and the mills humming. Now the Bank moved from threats into action, tightening the financial screws on the South, the West, the East. It refused money to Boston merchants to pay tariff duties on cargoes already on the wharves. It demanded all money due from the state banks. It drained cash out of the West to the East so fast that a kind of paper scrip called Jackson money went into circulation and people were hoarding coins. "Nothing but the excitement keeps me up," Jackson said.

In December Henry Clay moved, in a fiery speech to the Senate, that Jackson be censured for removing the Government deposits. Calhoun backed him up and spoke of the men who had removed the deposits as "pilferers under the silence of midnight." Even Daniel Webster supported the censure. The Senate debated for three months, then passed the resolution, 26 to 20. Immediately Benton moved that the Senate expunge this dark blot from Jackson's name. Jackson himself sent in a protest, but the Senate refused to receive it as a "breach of the privileges of the Senate." Again, without success, Benton moved to expunge.

Meanwhile the excitement was crashing about the President's head. Petitions inspired by Biddle were pouring in upon him. Delegations bore down upon him; Jackson dismissed them with brevity. "Go home, gentlemen, and tell the Bank . . . to relieve the country . . . I will never recharter the . . . Bank . . . Go to Nicholas Biddle."

Daily the President was receiving assassination threats. One congressman even charged that Jackson's famed Revolutionary exploits were only propaganda. "The damned infernal scoundrel," Jackson exploded, pointing to the scar on his forehead. "Put your finger there."

Someone spoke to him of "the people."

"The people! The people, sir, are with me."

In the House the young Speaker James Knox Polk dragged out the Bank debate with roll calls.

But at the White House Jackson kept his sense of humor. Once he put on a feathered Indian warbonnet, saying, "I don't think those fellows would like to meet me in this."

As 1834 began, it became apparent that the country could not long survive this duel between Jackson and Biddle. In February, the Pennsylvania Legislature, stung by Biddle's refusal to lend the state $300,000, voted to support Jackson's position; and soon after, New York broke with the Bank.

By March, the inevitable doom of the bank was clear; and in the end Jackson won, as he said, "a glorious triumph." In April, the House and then the Senate voted that his veto of the bill to recharter the Bank be sustained, and Clay's resolution of censure was tabled.

In fact the charter still had some time to run. It actually did not expire until 1836, but for all practical purposes the Bank was broken, although not its capacity to do harm. For if Jackson had declared war on the Bank, the Bank declared war on the country, suddenly calling in its loans and causing a drastic depression for lack of ready money across the land. Later the Bank relented and issued money in a stream. This, along with the "pet" or state banks springing up like mushrooms everywhere, sowed the country with paper currency and a wild inflation that boded badly for the future. But the battle of the Bank was over.

Meanwhile, a new joy had come into Jackson's life with the marriage of his son, Andrew, Jr., to a lovely dark-haired Quaker girl named Sarah Yorke, of whom he wrote: "I shall receive her as a daughter and cherish her as my child." In August of 1834, he returned to the Hermitage; and for his first "grandchild," little Rachel, he brought home in his arms a "pretty," a doll. This induced the shy child, "sprightly as a little fairy and as wild as a little partridge," to come to her grandfather. In the evenings when he was at the Hermitage, after his servant George had helped him into the long white nightshirt he wore, he would remove the miniature of Rachel from his neck and prop it on a table. Then Sarah would come in and read from Rachel's worn Bible to her "Father." She was the only one in the family to call him that.

But not all was well at home. Sarah had been a rich girl with a rich girl's tastes, and Andrew, Jr., was in debt. The cotton crop was poor. Though he remained in Tennessee only a month, Jackson himself directed the plowing of his fields and the planting of timothy. He left in September after writing ahead that the White House should be cleaned of bedbugs. Then the Hermitage was gutted by fire. Sarah managed to see that some of the

The first U.S. president to come from a poor farm family, Jackson fought for the rights of "plain folk" throughout his two terms in office.

furniture was saved, the President's papers, and Rachel's clothes which her husband had long treasured. The public wanted to take up a collection to rebuild the dwelling, but Jackson stopped this. "I am able to rebuild my home," he said.

Then one of the frequent threats almost came true. Jackson attended a funeral in the capital. As he was walking out, he came face to face with a small dark man who whipped out a pistol and leveled it at the President's chest. Jackson went taut. The trigger clicked. Jackson remained standing, then went for the man with his cane. "What! What is this, sir?" he demanded.

The man dropped the pistol, pulled out another, and fired again. Jackson still stood, and someone crashed the would-be assassin to the floor.

"He missed me both times," the President said, wonderingly. He had. Each pistol had misfired, and the mathematical chances of this happening and of the President's surviving were about 1 in 125,000.

This was worse, far worse than Jackson's previous encounter with a fanatic who wanted only to yank at the Presidential nose. Though Jackson calmly ordered that his would-be assassin be confined and given a fair trial, he was convinced that "the minions of the Bank" were behind this obvious "plot" to murder him. There was no plot. The man was insane, possessed of that mentality, peculiar to assassins of Presidents, which had led him to believe himself God's instrument to rid the country of a gross tyranny. He furthermore thought he was the rightful heir to the throne of England.

Completely undisturbed, Jackson was discovered at home that evening laughing and feeding candy to the White House babies. His greatest joy now was the warm family life about him. Grimly, he would endure the formalities of state dinners with thirty-two candles blazing in their chandeliers and course after course brought in— French soup, beef bouille, boned wild turkey, cold chicken, tongue and "salled," canvasback ducks with celery, partridges and sweetbreads, pheasants and Virginia ham, with dessert of jelly and little tarts, dried fruit, preserves, ice cream and fruit. The French servants, under the direction of the chef, knew how to serve each course sparingly, so that every dish at least could be tasted.

But affairs such as this interested Jackson far less than family holidays, such as the Christmas when he had told the White House children that Santa Claus had never visited him when he was a boy. They pled with him to hang up his stocking along with theirs. The next day someone found him in tears over the corncob pipe, the tobacco and the trinkets the children had stuffed into his stocking.

Andrew, Jr.'s, family visited him in Washington. "Grandpa, the great fire burnt my bonnet," little Rachel said. Sarah went shopping for replacements to her own wardrobe and ran up a bill of $345 which the President paid. He faced life as it came to him.

It was 1836 and his term was nearing a close. Once again the country was booming with prosperity. There was a huge surplus in the Treasury, which Jackson feared might be misused, so he distributed it in the form of "loans" to the states. None of them was ever repaid, and many officials simply helped themselves.

But in spite of the surplus, signs in the economy were troubling the President. The boom was too big. Paper money was floating about like snowflakes. Prices were too high, and even poor workmen were losing their hard-earned life's savings in various fly-by-night gambling schemes. Worst of all was the wildcat speculation in the new land to the West. Paper towns on paper maps, imaginary towns with imaginary roads and imaginary public buildings were paid for with paper money.

Jackson decided to put a stop to the business. He issued the so-called Specie Circular, demanding that all public lands be paid for in good solid coin. Again, as with the National Bank, he knew what was wrong; but he did not know what to do to make it right. The Circular should have been issued eighteen months earlier. Now it was too late. All the hard money in the East now began to flow West. Once again, the country nosedived into depression. Before the end of 1836, nearly all the banks were closed. Mobs broke into the food warehouses; people starved silently in their homes. But no one blamed Andrew Jackson. Jackson would be out of office by the time the depression was at its worst, so the blame would be heaped on the blond head of his successor. In any event, the saying still went that "General Jackson's popularity can stand anything." Because the people knew that he was for them, they would forgive him anything.

Some unfinished business still remained. From the first years of his Presidency, Andrew Jackson had never taken his eyes off Texas. That this vast subcontinent of a nation would become a part of the American Union, he had never doubted. He even felt that the United States had a claim to the territory, according to the old lines of the Louisiana Purchase. For years Americans had been drifting into Texas, actually encouraged by the thinly settled Mexicans who welcomed the hard-shooting Texans' help against the Indians. By the 1830's there were more than 20,000 Americans in Texas. Among them was the ever-venturesome Sam Houston, from whom Jackson had extracted a "pledge of honor" not to follow Aaron Burr's old dream and seek the throne of Mexico. But another dream might be fulfilled . . .

In the cluttered White House study, Jackson had mused over reports from Houston that Mexico was torn by civil war, that the people of Texas were "determined to form a state government." Settlers were bringing more guns than plows. And now the news was coming in quickly.

War broke out in 1836. Texas riflemen had thrown the Mexicans back over the Rio Grande. They had captured San Antonio, adopted a constitution, and elected a President. Then came the tragic roster of defeat and massacre: Goliad, San Patrico, and a sun-baked, blood-soaked, little fortified church called the Alamo. Here the legendary Davy Crockett and Jim Bowie had laid down their lives.

More news came. Sam Houston had been named Commander-in-Chief of whatever army he could find. For days he had zigzagged and retreated back and forth among the burned homesteads and widowed women and orphaned children, picking up men here and losing them there. He was "the last hope of Texas." He was leading the Mexican commander a wild chase up and down the whole vast area, forcing Santa Anna to split off sectors of his army. Sometimes the Americans could even hear the Mexicans singing the "Deguello," the ferocious beheading song. It had been played at the Alamo. Wild reports poured in as Jackson frowned over the map in his study.

Then the incredible, unbelievable word came. After thirty-eight days, Houston and his men had met the army of Santa Anna on the banks of the San Jacinto River. They had charged to the cry of "Remember the Alamo!"; they had fought; Houston had dropped with his chest raked and his leg shattered. But the Americans had won. They had smashed the Army of Mexico and taken Santa Anna prisoner. Bursting with pride over Houston, Jackson thought San Jacinto an even greater victory than New Orleans, for at New Orleans he had only defended; Houston had attacked. "The sheer splendor of one man's leadership had wrought a miracle in the history of warfare."

If only Jackson could bring Texas into the Union. But Texas was still claimed by Mexico and

Spain. And Jackson, despite all the impetuosity his enemies charged him with, also hesitated. It was the last year of his presidency. Although there were only a few slaves in Texas, the Southern slaveholders and nullifiers were making the cause of Texas their own. Day by day they were equating the annexation of Texas with the preservation of slavery. The cry for abolition was sounding in the North; the Abolitionist poet John Greenleaf Whittier wrote of "slave-accursed Texas." The Abolitionist torchbearer William Lloyd Garrison thundered that all those who wanted Texas to become American "hate liberty and would dethrone God." So, although Texas and Houston were clamoring for annexation, though Jackson knew that he should have the glory, he held off. To annex Texas would be to drive a wedge between North and South, fan anew the very flames of disunion that he had stamped out before. For this time the cries against the Union would come from the Northern states. So all Jackson had been able to do was grant official recognition to the young Republic on the last day of his term.

11

The Last of Triumph

JACKSON'S ADMINISTRATION was ending in triumph. His program had been accomplished. The Bank was destroyed. Nullification was put down. The Indians had been herded west. The Democrats were in control. Furthermore, France had paid her debt to the United States and this last victory had been achieved with characteristic Jacksonian dash and recklessness.

The French debt dated back to the War of 1812. During those years when Britain was mistress of the seas and Napoleon master of the Continent, American citizens and American shipping had been the victim—of both sides. To retaliate for these wrongs was a good part of the reason why we fought the War of 1812. But it had not been good politics then to challenge America's old ally, France. Americans had been held in French jails under suspicion of being British. American ships had been confiscated because the British had forced them to enter one of their ports. After years of dickering, the French had finally admitted that America had claims, but there was no agreement as to the amount of the claims.

Now the Revolution was a long distant memory. A mild hint by Jackson of "possible collision" between the two powers and one of France's quick changes of government at last resulted in negotiation. The sum set was $5 million. This was agreed to in 1831. A treaty was ratified, but somehow, France failed to find the money. When the issue was raised again the King was willing, but the Chamber of Deputies simply refused to vote the sum.

Years had passed and Jackson had had enough. France had delayed for twenty-five years. "It is not to be tolerated," the President said, "that another quarter of a century be wasted in negotiations."

So Andrew Jackson laid down the law. If immediate payment was not forthcoming, he would authorize "reprisals" involving the seizure of "French property in the United States." His language was polite enough, but diplomatically speaking this threat had but one meaning—war. France broke off relations, outraged. Paris went wild. Determined to enforce American "rights,"

Jackson delivered a five-day ultimatum—pay up, or he too would break off diplomatic relations. "I know them French," he remarked. "They won't pay unless they're made to."

The French demanded an apology; he would give none. Suddenly, on the floor of the House of Representatives, old John Quincy Adams, Jackson's onetime supporter and longtime enemy, arose and urged every man who was an American to stand behind his President. Next England offered to mediate the dispute, and the offer was accepted. On May 10, 1836, the official announcement was made—the French debt was paid.

It was in the blaze of glory after this affair that the loyal Thomas Hart Benton determined to bring about a final sweet triumph for the outgoing Administration. Benton had taken to the country the question of the Senate's censure of the Chief Executive for the removal of the Bank deposits. Passionately, he had demanded that the black mark against the President's name be removed, and that the Senators who had voted for it be defeated. Several of them were. The time came at last when Benton knew that he had the votes. He spread a victory feast in the Senate cloakroom for celebration—afterwards. Among those not invited were Henry Clay and John C. Calhoun, who was all in black, "as if in mourning for the Constitution." By a vote of 25 to 19 the censure was expunged and crossed out in black ink.

By this time, of course, Martin Van Buren had been chosen President of the United States. He had been handpicked by Jackson. He had been elected easily and uneventfully over the Whig candidate, the aging General William Henry Harrison. Jackson was particularly grateful that he would have the pleasure of seeing sworn in as President a man rejected by the Senate as an ambassador, and to be sworn in by a new Chief Justice, that same Roger Taney whom the Senate had rejected as a Cabinet officer.

Yet sadness shadowed Jackson's last weeks in the White House. He was greatly concerned over the depression darkening the country. He had had a dream of death, but not his. Emily Donelson was ill; Emily, the lovely, gay-spirited hostess of his first White House years, who had pitted her courage against the courage of her uncle. She was now twenty-eight. Jackson had sent her husband Jack home to beautiful Tulip Hill, the house he had built them as a peace offering after the Peggy Eaton affair. She had had her bed drawn to the window so that she could watch for her husband's arrival. But when he was two days away, she said goodbye to her children, turned aside, closed her eyes, and died. "Emily, farewell,"

Jackson had written. He was saddened, too, over stories of the Eatons drifting back to him from the Court in Spain, of John drinking heavily and Peggy smoking cigars.

Three weeks more. . . . He spent most of his time in bed now. Once in a while he put on a robe and dragged himself to the couch in the study, "strewn with official papers." Even to sign his name threw him into a dripping perspiration. As he struggled to write his final message, a hemorrhage ripped at his lungs and blood poured from his mouth. But he had to pen his last Annual Message, to issue a final warning: "The Constitution cannot be maintained, nor the Union preserved, in opposition to public feeling, by the mere exertion of . . . coercive powers. The foundations must be laid in the affections of the people."

Farewell gifts were pouring in upon him: a wagon, a carriage made of wood from the U.S.S. *Constitution*, and a 1400-pound cheese. This he served at the last levee, where draymen and shop girls, diplomats' wives and Cabinet ladies crowded for a sad goodbye to the man who had brought the blessings of democracy to them all, rich and poor alike. The President dressed, came downstairs and bowed.

On the evening of March 3rd, Jackson drank a

toast to the new young Republic of Texas. Quiet in his own room at last, he read a chapter from Rachel's Bible. His servant George snuffed out the candle.

March 4th was clear and almost warm. For only the fifth time since November, Jackson left the White House. He rode beside Van Buren in the *Constitution* carriage, as the massed thousands looked on. They started a cheer; it broke in their throats. As if in one gesture, all hats came off instead. "For once, the rising was eclipsed by the setting sun." Then, as Benton noted, a great shout arose that "power never commanded." This was love, gratitude, adoration, and looking on, Benton felt the surge of an emotion he had never known before.

The Inauguration of Martin Van Buren was over. Halfway down the steps Jackson paused, took off his hat, and bowed once again to the people he had served. Humble to the end, he had left a forwarding address for his mail: "Hermitage, near the Fountain of Health," this being a popular resort of the day.

Van Buren had wanted him to stay on at the White House and rest, but Jackson would remain in Washington only two more days. On March 5th he dropped in on friends and summarized what he thought to be the outstanding events of his Presidency. The Bank—he was proudest of this; he had saved the people from a monopoly that might have seriously injured them. The tariff? Not so good; states' rights still smoldered. Texas—he wished he could have brought it into the Union, and Oregon should come next, all the way up to latitude 54:40. Did he have any regrets? Yes, he admitted to two. He wished he could have shot Henry Clay and hanged John C. Calhoun!

He left on March 6th, the Surgeon General, at Van Buren's orders, going along. Once again there were the people engulfing the railroad depot, flowing out onto the track. Jackson stood on a rear platform, holding his hat. Once again, the wind tossed his white hair. He did not speak; the people made no sound. As the steam hissed and the cars began to move, Jackson bowed to the people for a last time. Then he vanished into the smoke. As it dissolved, it seemed "as if a bright star had gone out of the sky."

The trip was a slow one over the blue mountains and the brooding dark hills of east Tennessee. The way was long, and there were the waiting thousands who wanted to do him homage along the road. Many now believed he would never survive the long journey home. But he did and the welcome in Nashville was tremendous. There were the familiar landmarks: the

Cumberland, tawny and broad as he had first seen it nearly fifty years before, when he arrived as a raw young lawyer. The Stones River was the same and Mill Creek, the pale blue hills fringing the sky, and the gently rolling bottom lands. Spring was bursting into bloom as he arrived; yet the aging Jackson knew that even in November, the ruby red of the dogwood leaves would still gleam, and the oaks would stab the gray drabness with points of golden light.

12

Texas

HOME AT LAST. Journey's end. The Hermitage. But this stately mansion, gleaming with whitewash across the front was not the simple home he had shared with Rachel, where every footstep would have brought back an aching memory. The fire had gutted the interior, and in the rebuilding, Sarah Jackson had realized that her father-in-law would never be a private citizen again, and that the dwelling must befit the dignity and position of a former President of the United States.

Jackson himself had designed the original solid, simple house of four rooms on each floor, two on either side of a broad central hallway that swept to a soaring spiral staircase, delicate as a twist of ribbon. Wings now were added on either side, on the left a spacious dining room, dominated by a long mahogany table on which were set the plain, heavy silverware and the gold-banded white china used at the White House. The right wing included what came to be a nursery for the growing family of grandchildren, with an office for Jackson across the hall, opening out of his bedroom. Here were his desks and bookcases, a chair made from wood from the U.S.S. *Constitution*, the marble-topped table at which he had written the directives he had issued at the Battle of New Orleans.

Now, he could keep close at hand the trophies cherished by a former President: his Masonic apron and manual, the gold swords presented him after New Orleans; the wax candle found in Cornwallis' tent the night of his surrender to Washington, which Jackson lighted on every anniversary of New Orleans; his ruler, on which were engraved the outstanding events of his life; his peace medal, and his Congressional medal; a pipe from the Alamo, a set of Mexican leggings from Sam Houston; his papers, pamphlets and proclamations, all carefully saved from the fire, and his favorite canes.

Nor was all changed in the bedroom, where he now slept, overlooking the gallery. Upon awakening, his first gaze would fall on the portrait of Rachel, her shell vases and jewel case on the mantel below. On the dresser, beneath a cherished baby portrait of "little Rachel" were his wife's scent bottles and sewing box, also covered in shells. No, he would never forget. To the end, he kept her clothes and many of her trinkets: her beaded purse and gold-rimmed spectacles, her nightcap and workbag and the high pearl comb she wore in her hair. Cherished also were all he had left to help him remember his parents: a wooden hatbox carried by his mother, and a single stone from his father's lonely grave.

Dignity, graciousness, and peace—these were the hallmarks of the Hermitage. It was a gentleman's home, reflecting jointly the cultured tastes of Sarah and the instinctive good taste of Jackson. Rugged and homespun though he was, Jackson was "sensitive to culture" and even had "a flair for elegance." The Victorian furnishings were light and graceful, stately rather than ornate; almost daily he had taken part by letter in the planning and reconstruction of his home. He had personally selected the imported, scenic wallpaper for the front hall, depicting the travels of Ulysses. Yet, lest he grow too proud, in the rear of the Hermitage still rose the clay-chinked cabins of Hunter's Hill, with their splint-bottomed chairs and pine tables and spinning wheels—the kind of furnishings used by the slaves nearby. It was to this simple home that Jackson had returned after New Orleans. Here he had known his happiest hours with Rachel, and it was here that his eyes often rested and his memory lingered . . .

Unfortunately, all these improvements to the Hermitage cost money. Sarah had not stinted; she had ordered all at once eight matching mahogany four-poster beds, with dressers, and innumerable horsehair sofas. But it was Jackson who had to pay. He had arrived home with $90.00 in cash, and Rachel's picture and little Bible. The Presidency had cost him his lifesavings, and he had pledged his future cotton crop against outstanding debts in Washington. As they had that earlier elder statesman, Thomas Jefferson, guests would almost eat him out of house and home.

Fortunately, he was a good farmer, and the dark earth spraying back from the plow would produce for him now, as it had in the past. But Andrew, Jr., was no farmer at all, and had piled up tremendous debts. His father was not legally responsible, but he believed himself to be, and bankruptcy was something Andrew Jackson never thought of.

So he mortgaged the Hermitage. He sold his fillies; he even sold his riding mare and the meat out of his smokehouse. He had hoped, upon returning home, only to gain strength enough to ride over the farm, and to quietly superintend the setting out of the cedars along the drive.

He gave up hopes for a quiet Christmas and made a laborious journey to New Orleans to raise money for his adopted son's debts. It was the year of the twenty-fifth anniversary of the Battle of New Orleans, and Martin Van Buren had thought it would be a spur to the Democratic cause if the General were a part of the celebration. So, almost too ill to stand, he endured ten nights and days of speeches, merrymaking, shouting, and fireworks. "I have found that complaining never eased pain," he said. Dimly, he looked out for the last time on that empty field where once the bayonets had pulsed in shimmering waves of life and death.

Death . . . life . . . his primary interest now was in the young lives coming along, the grandchildren, and grand-nieces and nephews whose future must be thought of. At the Hermitage, as at the White House, he would pace the corridors in old-fashioned white nightshirts and gaily patterned dressing gowns, mindful of the children's sleep, their croup, their cries. Often it was he who walked the floor with a crying baby, while the mother slept.

His fourth "grandchild" was born, and Jackson wondered if this boy would live to help "save our glorious Union." He would never know that the baby's two older brothers would fight against the Union for the Southern Confederacy. But not this boy . . . Jackson was looking on as the baby was taken lifeless from the arms of his sobbing mother Sarah. So many he had known were gone: the old comrades-in-arms and the gallant, courageous women, "sweet Emily" Donelson, and the beautiful young wife of Andrew Jackson Hutchings, who was now battling the tuberculosis that finally killed her. And Rachel . . . time and again, Jackson would steal out through the pungent box hedges to the formally patterned flower garden she had so dearly loved. In this garden where his beloved lay, he would sit for hours beneath the magnolia trees. All his triumphs, all his fame and his power, he had once told a friend, he would exchange if she could be restored to him for a single moment. But it would not be long now. Often, "from affliction and debility" he was literally gasping for breath. Soon he knew he would join Rachel in the tomb.

Others, too, were aware of this. But he refused to let his remains "BE THE FIRST IN THESE UNITED STATES TO BE DEPOSITED IN A SARCOPHAGUS MADE FOR AN EMPEROR OR KING." This offer was made to him by a Naval commodore who had brought the emperor's coffin over from Palestine. But Jackson politely assured him: "I have prepared a humble repository for my mortal body." Meanwhile, he had yet one more battle to fight.

Thwarted as a state, Texas had decided to go

on as an independent nation. It had a capital of unpainted, shacklike stores and false fronts. This was Washington-on-the-Brazos, seared by hot wind and flying dust. It had a Senate that met upstairs over a liquor store, and an "Executive Mansion" of two rooms built of logs. It had a President, big Sam Houston, sometimes in Indian dress, sometimes in black velvet, receiving in the dog trot of the "Mansion" as he shaved in the mornings.

Houston was, as a discerning Spaniard once said, "a very deep and subtile man." He had never given up his dream of bringing Texas into the American Union, and he was convinced that Jackson had not, either. But how could this be done? For eight years he ran the affairs of the lusty young Republic. Now it was 1844. Three times Texas had knocked at the door of the Union and three times been refused. Now, in his exasperation, Houston determined upon a dangerous game: to play upon the fears of the dying Andrew Jackson, to play England, France, Texas, and the United States off against each other, blackmail the Union into annexing his country. Would the United States stand by and see Texas fall prey to a land-hungry overseas power?

It was part of his plan that Jackson know what was going on. Heartsick, the old chieftain read the carefully calculated warnings from Houston, whom he loved as a son. If forced to the wall, Texas might even lure the South into disunion. Then, together they would seize the Pacific coast and build a great "rival power" west of the Mississippi river. United with the South on slavery, Texas could exist without the United States, but could the United States exist without Texas?

Now Houston began flirtations with foreign powers. The young Republic must have a protector, and a dark rumor, skillfully concocted by Houston, was afloat; Texas would ally itself with England. Wounded to the quick, Andrew Jackson was roused to one last mighty effort as Houston had known that he would be. In mental and physical agony, the old man warned Houston that he must not "become the dupe of England," and urged a last final drive for annexation.

Texas, it was clear, would be the issue of the Presidential campaign of 1844. It was also clear that Henry Clay would run again and that he would dodge taking a stand. Who then would be the Democratic candidate? Not Van Buren; he was against annexation. "Why not Jimmy Polk?" Jackson asked. He had been the very embodiment of compromise and moderation during his years as Speaker of the House. Yet he was all-out for Texas; that was enough. It was Polk, "Young

Hickory," who suddenly became the most available man. He won Southerners by calling for Texas and Northerners by calling for Oregon; Clay, as usual, was for the middle and moderation. "It will be close," Jackson warned.

Goaded by Houston's shocking, stinging communications, the former President startled the nation with fiery communiques of his own. It was his last great year. His was the task, the challenge, to arouse the momentum of public opinion and see brought into the American Union the greatest empire since the Louisiana Purchase. So he wrote, in shaky wavering handwriting, to his old friends, his old supporters, his old military comrades. All over the nation flowed his passionate appeals. The newspapers printed them. The people read them and light flashed in their eyes. This was it. This was Old Hickory again.

The groundwork was laid now. Jackson's thread of life was spinning out to the end, but he kept on writing. When he was too weak to hold a pen, he dictated with closed eyes. Once again, a Treaty of Annexation lay before the Senate; Jackson now warned individual Senators that unless it were ratified, Texas would be driven into the arms of England. Texas was "the key to our future safety." Meanwhile, the election returns were coming in with agonizing slowness. Slowly, with some 2,600,000 votes cast, the decision for Texas came clear. Polk had won by a scant margin of 38,000 votes.

The President-elect hastened to Washington to add his weight to the drive for annexation. John Tyler, too, the retiring Chief Executive, was doing his part. He had called Jackson's old enemy, John C. Calhoun, out of retirement to head the State Department, for the express purpose of bringing Texas into the Union. "I'm glad Mr. Calhoun got right," Jackson said. Like Houston, the South Carolinian had seen to it that Jackson was sent a newspaper article hinting that England would seize Texas if the United States did not, and Jackson had flashed back that as a nation we were bound to protect Texas. Now the long fight was almost over. Calhoun worked out a treaty, but could not get the required two-thirds vote in the Senate because of agitation over the slavery question. Undaunted, he tried another way. Texas was annexed to the United States by a joint Resolution of the two houses of Congress, requiring only a simple majority vote.

"The pressure of two Presidents and an ex-President is too much for us," the opposition confessed. The night before he had left Tennessee for Washington, President-elect Polk had stayed at the Hermitage, and he and Jackson had talked

This photo portrait was taken by Mathew Brady, the famous Civil War photographer, seven days before Jackson's death in June 1845.

late about Texas. Said Jackson now, upon hearing the news: "I congratulate my beloved country."

There was still one more obstacle to hurdle: Sam Houston. Texas had had to "go begging," as Houston had sneered in his farewell address as Chief Executive. Now, she might even refuse annexation. Perhaps it was already too late. Houston's pride had been buffeted and trampled, and now, as he went, so would go the Republic of Texas.

Sick at heart, Jackson heard that his old friend was hesitating. What would Houston do? he wondered. He wrote him: "I congratulate you, I congratulate Texas." But not until May 26 did the news come that he was waiting for. A letter arrived from Sam Houston. Jackson read it and sighed. "All is safe at last." Texas would ratify the Treaty of Annexation.

Now Jackson was free to seek in death the peace he had never known in life. "British gold could not buy Sam Houston," he exulted. Houston was on his way to the Hermitage to bring the good news in person, but Jackson had little hope that he would live to see him. "My lamp is nearly burned out," he confessed.

13

Death of a Hero

DEATH WAS ADVANCING upon Andrew Jackson, slowly, mercilessly. "Pain was never absent for a day and for the last two years hardly for an hour." Hemorrhages prostrated him; dropsy had set in. But he never complained; he was Andrew Jackson still. Ill as he was, any man less than Jackson could not have endured a week. Would the General go to Heaven? one of the slaves wondered.

"He will, if he wants to," the confident answer came.

He spent his nights propped up in bed, his days in the study in an invalid's chair, which had been made for him with wide side arms and a leg- and foot-rest, all upholstered in green velvet. His Bible, Rachel's prayer-book, his writing materials and newspapers were close at hand. Even now, there were few quiet days: the problems of crops, livestock, and politics were continual and pressing.

The parade of peaceful pilgrimages to the Hermitage went on. All who came were struck by the tragic dignity of the stately man in the invalid's chair. George Healy, the artist, came to paint a last portrait, and Michael Brady came with his camera. All who saw him felt his fascination. All knew they were looking their last upon Andrew Jackson, who somehow had made himself one with the greatness of his great country. To many he *was* the United States of America.

He had overdramatized himself and overexaggerated everything that had happened to him. As Gerald Johnson has written, he had made insolence out of Spanish indolence, bribery and corruption out of Henry Clay's playing politics, a monster out of the United States Bank, a devil out of John C. Calhoun, and an angel out of the woman he loved. Yet the very intensity with which he felt and saw, dramatized the causes that he believed in and made them the people's own.

Because of him, a changed America was ebbing from his dying view. Because of him, the Redcoats were swept into the sea. Because of him, the common man walked with a new dignity, and shared with the uncommon man the power and the privileges of a free America. Because of him, the Union had been preserved, and the office of the Presidency endowed with strength and authority it had never known before. In addition, it had become the tribunal of all the people.

Andrew Jackson had done for the people what they had dreamed of doing for themselves. Because of this, the people loved Andrew Jackson; they worshipped him, and the author Herman Melville would invoke God thus: "Thou who didst pick up Andrew Jackson from the pebbles; who didst hurl him upon a war-horse; who didst thunder him upon a throne." All that the people could give they gave to Andrew Jackson, and all that they gave he accepted with grace and humility. But now it was time to say farewell . . .

On Sunday, June 1, 1845, he asked his family to go to church. This might be "the last holy Sabbath" he would be with them. The next day the pain was so great he prayed to God for strength to help bear it. Drugs were given and by Friday he was quite "comfortable," and wanted to write a letter to President Polk. His son suggested that he wait until tomorrow. "Tomorrow I may not be here," Andrew Jackson said.

He wrote the letter, his signature sprawling and long.

In his great biography of Jackson, Marquis James gives the most moving account of the old warrior's last hours, drawing on the correspondence of Andrew Jackson, Jr., to fill in the details.

Sunday June 8th dawned hot and still as James tells it. The doctor arrived to find Jackson erect in his invalid's chair, a servant on either side of him. One look at that stark face and the doctor ordered him back to bed. There he quietly fainted away.

But he revived, said goodbye to the servants, kissed and blessed each member of his family. From his neck he took the miniature of Rachel and put it around the neck of little Rachel, bidding her to wear it "always." Then, as muffled sobs broke out, he promised them all that he would meet them in heaven, "both white and black."

The yard was filling with people now; more slaves were filing in from the fields. Peggy O'Neale and John Eaton were there. Another friend arrived and entered. "You had like to have been too late," Jackson said.

Where was Sam Houston? Would he never come? Jackson whispered a message for him and for Tom Benton. His tired ears heard the moaning cries from outside. "Oh, do not cry. Be good children and we shall all meet in heaven." His eyes closed; the chanting died away. The majestic white head drooped to the side; the breathing stopped. Andrew Jackson was alone with his glory.

An hour or so later came the sound of gallop-

A bronze statue of "Old Hickory"—frontier general and seventh president of the United States—stands in the U.S. Capitol Rotunda.

ing horses and a carriage rolled up before the Hermitage. Down stepped a very tall man holding a little boy by the hand. The people fell back; they recognized Sam Houston. When he saw Jackson, white and still as a statue, he dropped to his knees. Sobbing, he buried his face in the dead leader's chest.

Then he arose and drew the boy to the bed. "My son," he said, "try to remember that you have looked on the face of Andrew Jackson."

Two days later, they laid him beside Rachel in the garden. The inscription on his tomb read:

<blockquote>General Andrew Jackson
Born March 15, 1767
Died June 8, 1845</blockquote>

That was all. It was enough.

For Further Reading

Chidsey, Donald Barr. *Andrew Jackson, Hero.* Nashville: Thomas Nelson, Inc., 1976.

Gatell, Frank Otto, and McFaul, John M. *Jacksonian America, 1815–1840.* Englewood Cliffs, NJ: Prentice-Hall, 1970.

Orinski, Alice. *Andrew Jackson.* Chicago: Childrens Press, 1987.

Schlesinger, Arthur M., Jr. *The Age of Jackson.* Boston: Little, Brown, 1950.

Viola, Herman J. *Andrew Jackson.* New York: Chelsea House, 1986.

Index

Abolition, 143
Adams, John Quincy, 37, 75; defends Jackson's actions in War of 1812, 76, 77; reaction to idea of Jackson as president, 82, 84; defeats Jackson, 86; Jackson's dislike for, 87, 89; defeated by Jackson in 1828, 89; leaves Washington, 94; praises Jackson proclamation, 121; annoyed at Jackson's Harvard degree, 127; urges support of Jackson's position on the French debt, 146
Alamo, 141, 142
Arbuthnot, 76, 89
Armbrister, 76, 89

Bank of the United States, 98, 117, 128-35, 144
Benton, Jesse, 42-43
Benton, Thomas Hart, 42-43, 99; in Jackson's "kitchen cabinet," 109; sympathetic to states' rights, 114; wins expungement of censure of Jackson, 146-47

Biddle, Nicholas, 98, 128-29, 131-34
Blair, Francis, 109
Blount, William, 26
Bowie, Jim, 141
Bowlegs, Chief Billy, 76
Brady, Michael, 165
Burr, Aaron, 27, 33-36, 39-40, 80, 100, 141

Calhoun, John C., 22; orders to Jackson, 75; angry at Jackson's seizure of Spanish territory, 76; candidate in 1824, 82; dropped as running mate by Jackson, 108; author of South Carolina "Protest," 113; Jefferson Day dinner speech, 114; Jackson's final break with, 115; elected Senator in 1832, 117-18; and the fight over nullification, 117-20; supports censure of Jackson, 124; and the expungement of Jackson's censure, 133; Jackson's dislike of, 161
Chesapeake, 38

Claiborne, Governor William C., 34
Clay, Henry, 77; Jackson's hatred of, 77, 86; candidate for presidency in 1824, 81; and Adam's election, 86-87; chosen Secretary of State, 87; and election of 1832, 116-17; compromise tariff plan, 122; moves censure of Jackson, 124; and expungement of Jackson's censure, 133; to run in 1844, 159
Cochrane, Admiral Sir Alexander, 59
Code of Honor, 21, 29, 31
Coffee, General John, 47, 48
Crawford, William H., 82, 83
Creek Indians, 43-44, 47-52
Crockett, Davy, 46, 141

Dickinson, Charles, 31-32, 89
Donelson, Andrew Jackson, 73, 79
Donelson, John (Jack), 73, 100
Donelson, Rachel, 17-20; *later* Jackson, Rachel Donelson, 28, 33, 68-69, 73-74, 78, 79, 84-85, 89, 90-92, 101, 105, 106, 125, 152, 153, 157, 167
Downing, "Major Jack," 127
Duane, William J., 132

Eaton, John, 94, 97-98, 103-05, 108, 109, 148, 167
Eaton, Peggy O'Neale, 103-08, 115, 147-48, 167
Election of 1832, 116-117

Fort Barrancas, 55
Fort Bowyer, 54
Fort Marks, 75

Fort Mims, 46
Fort Pitt, 82

Garrison, William Lloyd, 143
Gibbs, General, 67
Green, Duff, 114
Green, General Nathaniel, 12

Harcy, Captain, 59
Hamilton, Alexander, 22, 23, 25, 33-34
Harrison, General William Henry, 38, 52, 147
Hayne, Robert Young, 99, 112-13, 114, 119
Healy, George, 165
Hermitage, 28, 33, 34, 71-74, 79, 85, 87-88, 91, 100, 135, 137, 152-55, 161, 163, 165
Hill, Isaac, 109
Houston, Sam, 35; fights in Alabama, 50; resigns governorship of Texas, 100; wish to bring Texas into Union, 141-42; agrees to ratify Treaty of Annexation, 163; at Jackson's deathbed, 169
Hutchings, Andrew Jackson, 73, 89, 100, 157

Jackson, Andrew, birth and boyhood, 7-13; parents, 7-8; schooling, 8-9; mother, 8, 10, 12-13; during Revolution, 9-13; in prison, 11-13; ill with smallpox, 13; enters law office, 14; as prosecutor in Nashville, 17; Lewis Robards jealousy of, 18-20; marriage, 20; temper, 21; helps draw up Tennessee constitution, 23-24; first representative from

Tennessee, 24; as senator, 26–27; on bench of Superior Court of Tennessee, 27; becomes Major General of state militia, 29–30; duels to defend wife's name, 29, 31–32; and the trial of Aaron Burr, 35–36; views on the War of 1812, 37–38; goes to New Orleans with volunteers, 41; nicknamed "Old Hickory," 30; goes to Alabama to fight Indians, 44; deals with mutiny, 47; receives regular commission, 52; suffers ill health, 52; strike at Pensacola, 53–55; at New Orleans, 56–57; becomes national hero, 68; recovers at the Hermitage, 71; and Indian fighting in Florida, 74–76; hatred of Clay, 77; governor of Florida, 77; talk of his becoming president, 79; returns to Senate, 84; defeated in 1824, 86; and election contest of 1828, 87–89; and Rachel's death, 90–92; inauguration, 94–95; cabinet, 97–98; and distribution of spoils, 102; and the Indian problem, 110; and nullification, 111–16; final break with Calhoun, 115; and election of 1832, 116–17; second inaugural, 124; in New England, 125–26; and the Bank of the United States, 128–35; attempted assassination of, 137–38; issues Specie Circular, 140; and the Texas question, 140–41; and the French debt repayment, 144–46; final weeks in the White House, 148–49; returns to Tennessee, 150–52; financial problems, 155; at anniversary of Battle of New Orleans, 156; and the annexation of Texas, 160; final illness and death, 164–65

Jackson, Andrew, Jr., 69, 73, 89, 135, 139
Jackson, Hugh, 10
Jackson, Rachel, see Donelson, Rachel
Jackson, Rachel, (granddaughter), 135, 139, 153, 167
Jackson, Robert, 11–13
Jefferson, Thomas, 23, 27, 36, 39, 78, 81, 102

LaFitte, Jean, 58–59, 65
Leopard, 38
Lewis, Major William B., 80, 112
Lincoyer, 73, 89
Livingston, Edward, 27, 53, 67, 108, 120

Marshall, Chief Justice John, 95–96, 110

"Old Hickory," see Jackson, Andrew

Polk, James Knox, 109, 133, 159, 161

Robards, Lewis, 18–20, 89

Scott, General Winfield, 85, 119
Sevier, "Nolichucky Jack," 16, 29, 31, 106–07

Taney, Roger, 108, 132, 147

Van Buren, Martin, 88, 97, 99–101, 103, 107–08, 109, 119, 130, 131, 147, 149, 156, 159

Webster, Daniel, 93, 99, 112–13, 121, 122–23